The Journey

By
Keith Hearn

ISBN-13 978-1545441183
ISBN-10 1545441189

i

A New Life

Contents

Acknowledgements

Mum

Peter Peterson – Great Grandfather for starting the Journey

Rodmond Frederick Peterson – The Grandad I never got to meet

My brothers Michael and Garry

I would like to thank Linda Flaherty and Gus Stephens for kindly proof reading the book

I would also like to thank everyone for their continued support and faith in what I do.

Warning
This book contains strong adult language

Life is far too short, so make the best of the
opportunities life offers. Everyone has a dream so don't
allow others to extinguish the dream and
Just reach for the stars

Keith Hearn

INTRODUCTION

The book is a story of a family's journey which continues for several generations.

It is a journey that is interspersed with life's many struggles.

The story starts in a land far away, it was a time when the poor and the unfortunates lived their lives far removed from the rich and educated.

The language contained within this book has much cursing and profanity, it was the language of the time.
I hope the reader will find the story of interest also an enjoyable read.

Chapter 1 – A New Life

It was 1871 and Ole was deep in his own thoughts as he stared out onto the harbour from his kitchen window he had been watching as the wind had whipped off the sea within the harbour and as the storm battered the fishing vessels he could hear the wind crashing with such tremendous force against his house. It was lucky the walls of the house had been built wide to withstand the force of any storm that would slam into the village. The waves were cascading against the nearby cliffs which surrounded the fishing village. The storm had begun far out to sea the storm had eventually crashed into the nearest land mass. The fishing vessels had been sheltering from the storm within the protection of the natural harbour and they were tucked away from the full force of the storm. The fisherman had ensured the vessels had been battened down and secured within the harbour. Ole and his family lived in the village situated on Streymoy one of the many Islands that which make up the Faroe Islands the village of Vestmanna is protected due to its natural harbour and sometimes it would be hit by extreme storms that came off the North Atlantic the steep slopes surrounding the harbour roll down to the harbours edge the village houses cling to the sides of the slopes. The Faroe islands are situated of the far North West of Scotland the Islands are halfway between Iceland and Norway and they come under the Kingdom of Denmark Greenland is another Island which also come under the Kingdom of Denmark. In 1871 the population of the Faroe Islands was only fifteen thousand people including Peter's very recent birth the population stood at fifteen thousand and one. The Islands are extremely isolated the Islanders are totally self-sufficient and they needed to be. The Faroese language is like the Icelandic and the old Norse languages it is very distinctive. The food consisted of meat, Potatoes and some fresh vegetables mutton was the basis of most of the Islanders meals. Skerpijot was also very popular it is aged and wind dried mutton and it is extremely chewy and it helps to produce some extremely strong jaws. Most homes have drying sheds known as a hjallur. The main diet is supplemented by raestur fiskur a matured fish or grind og spik it is pilot whale meat with lots of blubber. Also, included in the Islanders diet was fresh fish and various seabirds for instance puffin and various bird's eggs. The diet was limited it was still far more superior and varied than anything the many of the poor of Great Britain were eating at the time. It was very difficult to travel from one Island to the many other Islands the main transport routes could only be accessible by boat. There wasn't much for the younger generation to do or to aspire to so it would mean many would move to mainland Denmark or as far afield as Great Britain. For many a young man, the main trade available to them was working at sea as fisherman and by working on the sea it would end up taking them away from the Islands and for months at a time and the fish caught would eventually end up being sold either in Scotland or further south England it all depended on the catch and the price the skipper would get for it. The Faroe fishing industry had purchased some of the old English and Scottish Brixham trawlers the very first boats had been built in Brixham but at some time, in the past they started to be built in many other parts of Britain they were of a wooden construction they had been built as a deep sea fishing trawler and there were two different sizes of boat between sixty and eighty foot in length they were sail powered and they had been snapped up at knock down prices by the Islanders they had eventually purchased many more of the fishing boats as soon as the English and the

Scottish fishing industry had fully converted to Steam driven fishing vessels and by purchasing the fishing vessels had enabled the Faroe fishing industry to grow so much stronger and so much more commercial. Before the Faroe fishing fleet had purchased the new fishing vessels they would have to fish by a more traditional method with only a line and hook each crew member would only be paid for every fish they had managed to catch. If a crew member became too ill and were subsequently unable to fish they would not get paid and there was no guaranteed work or any kind of insurance for any eventuality. The thought of fishing by line conjures up thoughts of a man fishing with a single line and a hook on the end and the line having been dropped into the sea it was far from it and by fishing with just a line it hadn't mean that they had fished with just a single line. The lines they were using had been made of one main line with approximately thirty smaller lines then attached to the main line. The whole contraption would then be dropped into the sea and hung from a buoy. There was so much time and effort taken to just bait the hooks once the lines had been in the sea for a while they had to be hauled up with their catch it had never been easy for the men to draw up a fishing boat alongside the buoys and then to try and pull the lines back onto the boats from the depths more than often many lines would have the catches taken from the hooks by much larger fish because the baited lines had been left in the sea far too long. It was an inefficient method of fishing. When the Faroe's fishing fleet had been upgraded with the Brixham trawlers most of the crews had come from the same village and it also included the skipper as he would know the crew's family he knew that he could trust the men he employed on his fishing vessel. Ole's wife Maren had recently given birth to their first child Peter. Ole was the village blacksmith and he was a highly skilled craftsman as he stood in the kitchen he was still looking out of the window and he could just make out the various fishing boats and they were still being tossed around just like toy boats and it had struck him "thank the gods I don't have to go out in one of those flimsy boats just to earn a living thank god not like the poor bastards who had to weather the seas". Maren called out from their bedroom their son Peter had been delivered by one of the local shepherds wives and she had done so over many years far too many to remember she had been used to helping her husband to deliver lambs there didn't seem to be so much of a difference between delivering lambs and delivering babies as long as the lamb or the babies heads were in the correct position for a natural birth and they weren't in a breached position because if the baby had become breached it would make for a very complicated and possibly a dangerous birth for both mother and baby. Their house was isolated on the steep hillside the village was also isolated from the other Islands there was only one doctor in the village and at the time of Peter's birth he had been assisting with another birth it was a potentially complicated birth. It could take hours or even days for another doctor to arrive from one of other islands. Maren was still a little sore and quite tender from the rigors of having recently given birth. Ole had let Maren know he was going outside to check on the state of the roof of the house because the roof had been constructed of turf and the earth sods were a traditional method and material which was used for the construction of the roofs of most of the houses the sods were a natural material to use and was extremely waterproof. Ole wanted to make sure that none of the turf sods had been damaged during the recent storm or had been ripped away from the roofing planks. The house had also been constructed from drift wood then it had been sawn into rough shaped planks and some of the houses in the village had been constructed of stone walls these were extremely solid buildings the stones had been gathered from the various beaches dotted around the harbour area. As previous mentioned most houses were constructed from planks of wood instead of the traditional roofing tiles turf sods had been lain on top of the tar treated planks of wood. There aren't any trees on the Faroe Islands and so the villagers collect the wood that has been washed up onto the beaches and the only flora growing on the Islands are the various arctic alpine plants, wildflowers, grasses, moss and lichen, hence the need to gather up any wood washed up on the shoreline as it provided much needed source of material to enable the local houses to be built far sturdier. The temperature in and around the Islands is constantly above freezing all year round due to the gulf stream. The village of Vestmanna sweeps down to a small harbour. The cliffs that surround the village are almost half a kilometre high. During the eighteen hundred's there hadn't been very much to do on the islands apart from surviving and attempting to eke out a meagre living. Ole had entered the house he had been soaked through to the skin at least everything on the roof looked ok as none of the sods had been ripped away from the roof during the worst of the storm the wind was still howling across the harbour. The wind was blowing a howler and the rain was coming down in horizontal sheets at least the roof had been checked as he couldn't afford to have Maren and Peter getting soaked from a leaking roof. As soon as he had stepped inside the house Maren shouted out "are you ok Ole is the house still ok?" He soon responded, "yes everything is safe and sound my love, I am going to put some more peat on the fire would you like some more broth?" she replied, "no I am fine, thank you sweetheart Peter has only just finished his feed and I have given him some breast milk" Maren was finding it very difficult to feed Peter using her own milk and so had begun to supplement her milk with some fresh dairy milk. Ever since

A New Life

Peter's birth Ole had been thinking about his future and more so his son Peter's future he really hadn't wanted Peter to have to go to sea to work as a fisherman fishing was far too dangerous there were far too many deaths due to the many accidents at sea it is extremely dangerous conditions that the fishermen would have to work under. He had come to the decision to teach Peter everything he knew about the blacksmith trade. Ole once again looked out of his kitchen window and at the view before him it was beautiful even with the storm raging outside. It was a bleak and sometimes a very dreary existence living on the Island Ole wanted so much more for his son even though Peter was still only a few days old. He was his son and heir and he already wanted the best for his son. He was so looking forward to the future as Peter lay in the next room with his mother. Ole had counted himself extremely lucky to be working as the village blacksmith his skills were in high demand and he was a highly skilled craftsman and he was the only blacksmith within the village. The fishing vessels were always in constant need of repair and that also included the many homes in the village even more so after a storm and some day's he would only make nails due to the constant repairs being made to the houses and once again more so after a storm just like the one that had smashed head on into the Island but on other days he would make various metal fittings for the many fishing boats he was constantly in demand to make iron fishing hooks for the local fishermen who would fish by the traditional method of hook and line. He often ventured out to scour the shoreline for any derelict boats sometimes a vessel would be scrapped and abandoned on the local beaches. Ole would help some other to strip the metal plating from the boats and would use the metal in his smithy he would sometimes melt the metal into various household goods such as pots, pans and kettles etc. Not everyone in the village had money at their disposal the coinage in the Faroe Islands was the Danish Krone those who didn't have access to money would use a type of bartering system it had suited Ole as he didn't have the time or the skills required to go out and hunt for food or to fish out in the choppy seas. Many of the repair works he carried out on a fishing vessel would be paid in fish rather than Krone for instance a fisherman may have provided fish over a monthly period and Ole would be guaranteed enough fresh food to help feed his family. A shepherd for instance would provide him with a sheep's carcase or some of the best cuts of meat to pay for his work bartering was used by a lot of people. If a fisherman was paid in Krone for his catch he would then be able to pay Ole in Krone, he rarely used Krone, he would keep any money that he had received securely in the house he would use the Krone whenever the family had a requirement to use cash and it would only be used in an emergency. For instance, if he needed cash to help raise Peter or to eventually help send him to school or if he had needed some specialised equipment for in the smithy. When Peter was five, Ole had begun to introduce him to the magical art of the blacksmith's trade on top of Peter's schooling and he would have to learn the basics of the blacksmith's trade, Ole taught Peter everything about the various blacksmiths tools the tools he would have to use in the workshop he would have to learn how the various tools were used. As Peter became older he would often wander around the small harbour and stand staring out towards the many boats moored alongside the quayside he would often go to the harbour and talk to the skippers about their adventures on the sea and Ole had soon realised he was becoming mesmerized by the fishermen's tall stories and their tales of how wonderful life was working on the seas and they would include stories of the many far off places that he could only dream about. The fisherman would continue to spin so many stories to a young and a very perceptible boy Ole had known his son was slowly but surely being drawn towards a life at sea. Peter was so young and he had believed that the grass was so much greener on the other side his father was so aware that his son would eventually want to become a fisherman and would eventually end up break his mother's heart. Ole would have to talk to Maren about his fears regarding their son's future and he would try to sow the seed in her head about the high probability of him joining the village fishing fleet and he would probably leave the village it would be his mother's worse nightmare. As Peter reached his teenage years he had become rebellious towards his father Ole had tried his very best to get Peter to show some interest in the Blacksmith's trade but he had known deep down his son would eventually join a fishing vessel the only thing was he didn't know when he would decide to leave. Ole like many other father's the world over he had only wanted the best for his son he and he had only ever wanted to guide him and to impart his knowledge he had developed during his own working life at the forge. During his teens Peter was totally mesmerised by the fishermen's sometimes farfetched stories of the sea and he had dreamt of a much better life his future was going to be as far away from the Faroe Islands as possible. One year a couple of foreign fishing boats had taken shelter from a severe storm far out at sea the fishing boats had sailed into the safety of the village harbour. Ole and Peter like most of the other people in the village had understood a little bit of English and these particular fishermen had travelled all the way from Grimsby in England, they had been fishing out in the North Atlantic when they were caught in the storm. Over the years, the villagers had been introduced to many English fishermen and many others who had sought shelter from the storms which so often batter the Islands some of the Faroes fishermen had sold their catches in Grimsby or Hull so they had been exposed to the English language and the people. The English fishermen had been made most welcome by the villages and Ole had invited three of fishermen to his home and when they were waiting for the storm to pass they had drank and had told tall stories about the many storms they had often encountered on their travels and of course young Peter was all ears he had taken each story to heart as this was his dream. The fishermen had kept an emergency supply of Danish Krone just in case of this kind of emergency. While the fishermen had stayed at Ole and Maren's home they would describe in detail the many places they had visited. He knew from his own experience not everyone would ever tell stories of their worst experiences they had ever encountered or about the realities of life. After a few days, the storm had died down sufficiently for the two English fishing vessels to venture out from the safety of the harbour. The skipper who had stayed at Ole's home during the storm had paid for his family's hospitality he had paid with Krone and it was a most welcome and generous gesture. The money had been much more than he would have seen in a whole year, Maren spoke in broken English telling the skipper the money was far too much and she had attempted to give some of the money back to the skipper but he had refused and said his goodbyes and left the family. He boarded his boat and headed out into the North Atlantic. Peter had followed the fishermen to the harbours edge he had stood on the quayside watching as the fishing boats had departed the harbour and headed out to sea. As he stood watching the vessels as they disappeared he knew one day he would travel to England and to the land of plenty. Ole knew he had already lost his son to the lure of the sea and he would have to accept the inevitable it was Maren that he had been most worried about not himself. Ole and Maren knew that their son Peter was drawn to a life on the sea and it would only be a matter of time before he would "escape the Islands". Ole had noticed more and more Peter was to be found hanging around the quayside and talking to some of the local skippers and the crewmen. There was one skipper he had observed Peter often spoke to and he knew each one of the skippers and the crews this skipper was called "Aksal" and he knew him extremely well as both of their families had grown up together he was a decent man. One morning Aksal had visited Ole in his blacksmith's workshop as he had needed some repairs to be carried out on his fishing vessel. Ole had greeted him and then asked him if everything was OK? At first Ole thought he had come to talk about Peter. He had decided to ask him outright what was the reason for his son to be talking to him at the quayside the skipper was a very straight talking man and replied "he had wanted to join him on his boat and he wanted to know when he was next going out to sea" Ole softly said "Aksal, Peter would never go to sea" he had pointed out Peter was over eighteen and if he wanted to join his crew he couldn't see any reason why he should say no? as it would be Peters choice. Ole replied "please it would break his mother's heart can't you just tell him that you have a crew and you don't need his services?". He replied, "I understand Ole I know my friend but that's life I am afraid" later that afternoon Peter had returned home and he had been out on the cliffs collecting eggs and down at a beach to collect seaweed and he had finished doing various odd jobs around the village to earn a little money. Ole and Maren were at home, Maren asked Peter to sit down and join them around the kitchen table. She pointed out to him they needed to have a very serious talk and Peter had a very good idea what it was going to be about. Ole spoke first he said "Peter your mother and I know all about your dreams and of you so desperately wanting to go off to sea, I have spoken to Aksal he has informed me of your wish to join his crew" Peter replied yes it is true I do want to join his crew and I also want to go to sea" Maren was very upset at this news and said "oh god no son, I will not let you go do you hear me" Ole replied "sweetheart there is absolutely nothing we can do as Peter is eighteen and a grown man". She turned to Peter and pleaded with him "son for the love of god please promise me you won't go to sea" Peter replied, "mother I can't promise you anything". It was at this point both Ole and Maren had finally realised their son would son end up going to sea but unknown to his parents he had already signed to join Aksal and his crew and on the boat, would be Peter's childhood friend Jorgen he too had signed to join the same crew. Peter had thought it would be better to keep what he had done a secret from his parents it had been bad enough his parents had found out that he was desperate to go to sea. Late one evening a lone fishing vessel slipped its mooring and slowly left the calm waters of the harbour it was to be the start of Peter's very long journey where to? At that precise moment, he didn't have a clue he would know better once they had arrived in England. Peter stood on board the fishing boat as it slowly sailed out of Vestmanna harbour. As Peter looked back towards the houses stretched out on the hillside he could just make out the lights flickering from some of the houses in the darkness Peter and he would never see such natural beauty ever again in his lifetime and from now on he would only see the dirt and grime of the industrial cities of England and the drudgery of working in the many docks of the north of England instead of the sights of the beautiful cliffs of Vestmanna instead he would only see the cathedrals of the great dock warehouses of England at that moment he was going to lose so much. He was very sorry to have deceived his parents and as he stood on the deck he thought he was about to make his dreams come true he was so excited but at the same time he was extremely apprehensive as to what the future held for him. The vessel had soon entered the choppy waters of the North Atlantic and it hadn't been anything he had imagined it would be soon the boat was being tossed about in the open waters very much like a toy boat. The crew had consisted of Jorgen, Peter, Boas, Jokil and of course the skipper Aksal. There was a slight twist unknown to the young men's parents both Peter and his friend Jorgen were working their passage to England and to the "Land of Plenty" at the time it had been the perception of many a young man from the Islands. They had thought of England as a country where their dreams could come true it was all due to the many tall stories they had been told by the many English sailors who had visited the Islands over the many years. It had been bad enough Peter was going to off to sea and for having disappeared in the dead of night and not having said a final goodbye to his parents and more especially his dear mother Maren he would never again get the chance to return to the Islands certainly not in his lifetime. It had been something his mother Maren had been so worried about as she had known plenty of other families whose sons had gone to sea and they had never returned it may have been that they had been killed at sea or something as simple as just staying in England or Scotland after a catch had been sold at a British dock and then to never to return to their homes. Meanwhile the fishing vessel was being tossed about in the heavy seas and was crashing against such huge waves that would crash onto the deck of the small boat. A few hours later the sea had become so much calmer and it was at this point the skipper had deployed the fishing nets and began to trawl the nets behind the boat the skipper had skilfully sailed the boat to an area where it was well known that there were huge shoals of cod and haddock he felt the shoal that he was chasing would turn out to be one of his most valuable of catches? Peter thought so far things had been fairly easy on board the fishing vessel and he was a strong and still very young so he thought he had no fear, that was until the waves once again crashed with great force onto the deck the bow headed straight into the waves and head on the boat was being tossed around in the sea it had felt just like riding a roller coaster the deck had been swamped with gallons of sea water the skipper had to keep the nets in the sea for as long as he could as he couldn't afford to pull the nets onto the deck just yet besides it would be extremely dangerous trying to fight the sea and at the same time trying to ensure the boat stayed upright and on an even keel and then to try and pull the many tons of fish currently caught in the nets it would be fool hardy of him as the safety of the crew was paramount and upper most in the skippers mind also at the same time his nets and the catch were on his mind as he could replace the nets but not his crew. He decided to drag the drift (Nets) for an hour or two until the sea had calmed down enough for the nets to be hauled back onto the boat it was still a little rough but not as bad as it had been it was at this point the skipper had instructed the crew to muster on the deck as he was about to winch the nets back on board as the nets were being winched he knew it was one of the most dangerous parts of the procedure to safely land the catch. As the nets were being dragged on board it looked as though things were going well and the skipper had looked at the nets and from where he was standing it looked like it was a very good catch and possibly a very profitable one. Peter and Jorgen were on deck with other members of the crew but on deck it was very cold and wet and it was extremely slippery on deck. As Jokil opened the net the catch had spewed out of the net and over the deck it had suddenly became even more dangerous on the deck there wasn't a grip on the surface. The fish were very slippery and there was very slimy sea weed mixed together with the catch and everything else that had been dragged into the nets was also

13

mixed together with the fish it made the deck extremely slippery and very dangerous it was a toxic mixture. It had been almost impossible to work on the catch they had to also free any fish and sea weed which was stuck in the gaps of the netting as they could not afford to reject any of the fish that were stuck in the netting it was such a valuable catch and there were a few hundred fish that had got caught in the gaps in the nets. Two of the crew had already begun to gut the fish and as they tried to throw the guts over the side of the trawler a lot of the guts and the innards had blown back onto the deck and had covered the men who were gutting the fish. The mixture added to the dangerous working environment the men were working in. Suddenly one of the crew members Boas had slipped on the extremely slippery deck and as he landed hard on the metal deck he had unfortunately smashed his head as he smashed onto the deck and at the same time and unknown to everyone working on the deck he had broken his neck. He had landed on the deck with such force his skull had smashed against the hard surface and he had ended up having cracked his skull open just like a raw egg with very similar results and only in a split second his neck had snapped and his death was instantaneous. The skipper had seen this kind of accident so many times before but for the teenagers they had never seen a dead person before it was a new experience it would be an experience they would experience more and more during their life time of working on the sea. The man who had been killed was very well known to everyone and he was very well liked. Peter was ordered by the captain to assist Jorgen and another crew member to recover the body before it was eventually washed overboard. Jorgen and Peter had struggled against the swell and the rolling of the boat to try to get to the body as soon as Peter saw the state of Boas's head he threw up over the deck the crew had struggled to wrap the body up inside a canvas tarpaulin laid out on the deck it was very difficult to wrap a piece of rope around the canvas and the body but after what seemed a mammoth struggle they had only just managed to drag the corpse inside the ships galley. His body was placed on top of the galley table and the captain ordered the crew to unwrap the body as he needed to look at it to confirm the time of death and write the details of his death in the ship's log they began to unwrap the body from the canvas. The captain checked the corpse ensuring he was dead when the body was unwrapped the crew could see that Boas had a massive gaping hole at the back of his skull some particles of his brain were oozing from the hole and spewed out onto the galley table. It was obvious to everyone present he was no longer breathing. As the captain Askal had to certify in the ships log that a member of his crew had died at sea and the details of how he had met his end. It was not a very nice task to carry out. Once he had written the circumstances of the death in the log the entry had to be certified as being true by all the crew members. Jacob and Peter were told by the captain to place some salt into the canvas and to wrap his corpse back into the canvas and once they had done so they then had to place his body into the hold and well away from the freshly caught catch. It took another day for the storm to subside and the remainder of the crew had fallen very silent and they had looked very sullen knowing that Boas's body had been wrapped in canvas and currently in the hold no wonder the moral of the crew was very low. It had been a very bad omen to have a crew member die on a fishing trip. Especially when the crew had been working together for many weeks and they had formed a bond it had been an extremely efficient team. Fishing in very dangerous and rough seas a crew quickly forms a very strong bond it is why a skipper knows he must choose the right men to crew his fishing vessel he would need men who would form a cohesive bond as he couldn't afford to have a crew member serving on his boat who wouldn't mix with the other crew members.

Chapter 2 – Land of Plenty

A lone fishing vessel had slowly made its way into the port of Grimsby the vessel looked rather battered and it was in a bit of a sorry state as the paint on the boat was peeling off from its hull the boat looked like it had been at sea for a very long time. It had slowly crept past the Grimsby Dock Tower and was heading for the Royal Dock it was 1891 the crew were standing on deck admiring the newly built dockside two of the crew Peter and Jacob were in awe at the sights appearing before their very eyes and of the sprawling dock yard spread out before them the friends had never visited England before and of course it was the very first time they had ever seen the Grimsby Port in fact they had never been outside of the Faroe Islands. As they gazed up at the tower in total disbelief before them was a huge industrial port and they could see just how busy the dockside was and there was the noise coming from the many steam engines and there were lots of cranes and were lifting tons of fish from the various holds of fishing boats and there were men shouting instructions to one another the various cranes were operated by a unique hydraulic system. The dock tower had been built to provide pressurised water to the cranes which enabled them to operate via the hydraulic system it was such an ingenious design and in the distance the cranes looked like they were picking up extremely heavy loads from deep within the holds of much larger ocean going ships from around the globe. Peter could see so many fishing vessels tied up in rows at the quayside it did look as though they were either waiting to have their cargo offloaded or they were waiting to obtain clearance to leave the docks and to travel out into the vast North Sea and out to the major fishing grounds. Again, he thought to himself that he had never seen the likes of it before the docks were such a busy place he just couldn't adjust his eyes to the enormity of everything before him he could see there must have been more people working at the dockside than the whole population of the Faroe Islands. Their vessel had been registered in the Faroe Islands and it wasn't an unusual sight within the Grimsby docks to have a fishing vessel arrive at the port from the Islands it was quite the norm. The fishing vessel had made a very arduous journey from the many fishing grounds in and around the Faroe Islands the vessel to some it had looked like it should never had been at sea in the first place even though it was a very sturdy boat with bags of character. The vessel and its crew had travelled from deep within the North Atlantic carrying its precious catch of cod and haddock it had to travel into the North Sea carrying their precious cargo it was a very valuable cargo and especially in the fish markets of Grimsby. Foreign registered fishing vessels many did not exceed the quotas of fish or would ever affect the British fish quotas there had been a British fisheries act at the time it was called The Sea Fisheries Act of 1868, the act listed the number of fishing vessels including the tonnage of each of the skippers had to register the port that they operated from and the class of the fishing vessel most of the British owners of smaller vessels never registered their fishing boats nor did most of the Faroes skippers the did not have to register their boats as the boats weren't anywhere close to the tonnage of the very large vessels. Grimsby was the best port in the country to offload a good catch a skipper was usually guaranteed the best price on the East Coast of England and with the advent of the Railways both Grimsby and Hull were then able to supply Billingsgate fish market in London. Askal had a buyer based within the Grimsby docks and he knew he would obtain a very good price for his catch but before he ever sold his catch he would walk through the Grimsby fish market to observe the price of the fish on sale and he would check on what the various catches were currently being sold for on the open market and if the catch of the day was of a poor quality or there hadn't been enough good quality fish caught to satisfy the market he would gauge the price he could receive for his catch. Onboard the fishing vessel the two friends who had together decided to seek their fortune were extremely excited at the thought of starting a new life in England. Peter and Jacob had heard so much about England and in their mind's, they had believed England was a land of plenty and a country where people could make their fortunes. They had recently been thrown headlong into the realities of a working life on the wild and the unforgiving sea on the voyage to Grimsby and unfortunately and they had witnessed one of the crew killed due to a very unfortunate and tragic accident. For the young men and having just arrived in Grimsby was going to be a totally different lifestyle than the one they had left behind. They had felt as though they had landed in a land where anything could be possible to achieve. Everything within the dockside looked so much bigger than the fishing village at home on the Faroe Islands. As soon as the fishing vessel was secured at the dockside the skipper had arranged for the mate to offload the catch and to take it to the Grimsby fish market and to sell the catch to the skipper's normal buyer the skipper entered the Town Hall and it was where the police station and the coroners court was housed. He went on to report the death of one of his crew. The police were used to investigating accidental deaths in the docks area also the many accidents which occurred onboard fishing vessels even if an accident had happened far out at sea. The police had a duty to carry out an investigation into every death and to report their findings to the coroner's office. Peter and Jacob had found rooms in Grimsby as the skipper had owned lodgings within Grimsby. As soon as the coroner's court had listened to the evidence from the crew and the Police evidence contained within the police's report it had concluded there had been a tragic accident which contributed to Boar's death. The coroner concluded his death had been deemed to be purely accidental and there were no suspicious circumstances. It was one of the many hazards of working at sea. His body was released into the care of the captain for onward transportation to the Faroe Islands and to his poor family for burial. The following morning Peter and Jacob were taken by their skipper to a Grimsby fishing skipper who had owned his own fishing vessel and he was looking for a couple of apprentices to serve on one of his fishing vessel it was steam driven and at the time it was state of the art. The English skipper took the pair on as apprentice fishermen the apprenticeship would last for over four years and both Peter and Jacob signed their apprentice contract documents. The English skipper had provided them with board and lodgings and the payment would be deducted from their miniscule wages they had moved out of Aksal's lodgings he would require them for a new crew having been apprenticed to a new skipper they at least had a roof over their heads and were provided with hot meals. At the end of his apprenticeship Peter would have earnt his licence to become a qualified fisherman in his own right. During his apprenticeship Peter had met a young local lass her name was Susan he had dated her throughout his apprenticeship when he first met Susan it was slightly difficult to communicate as he spoke very little English he didn't earn much money during his apprenticeship but love soon blossomed. Peter had first seen Susan at the quayside she was visiting her father George who was also a Fisherman through her father she had known what it was like to work at sea it had been extremely hard work it was a rough life working at sea. On the 12th of December 1895 Peter and his friend Jacob had finally gained their fishing licences it would mean if they had enough money they could buy their own Fishing vessel and have their own crew. Peter would never have the kind of money to be able to own his own fishing vessel instead he would have to find work with a skipper who owned his own boat. Jacob had soon settled in Hull and he had married a local girl and he had eventually saved enough money to purchase a fishing Trawler. Jacob and his wife soon had children and in the summer months he would trawl for fish in the North Atlantic and on the way to the fishing fields he would visit his family in the Faroe Islands. In the summer months, he would drop his wife and children off at the Faroe Islands while he went on to fish in the North Atlantic after many weeks of fishing he would stop off at the Faroe Islands to collect his family and bring the catch and his family back home to Hull. It must have been very exciting times and for Jacob's children it must have seemed like a great adventure. Peter himself had eventually married his sweetheart Susan and in 1896 they had settled in Stirling Street New Clee and they were extremely happy together Peter was ever so lucky to have found work onboard a fishing trawler even though it had been with a local skipper he had felt sad that is was not on a boat of his own, it was also the start of the bubble bursting regarding his hopes and dreams. Sometimes when Peter had found himself in between work for whatever reason he would sometimes work with Susan's father George he was also a fisherman and in the past Peter had worked with him on various trawlers. By 1896 Susan's Father had been killed due to a fatal fishing accident he had been working onboard a trawler way out in the North Sea. His body had been returned to the docks his untimely death had been reported by the skipper of the fishing vessel to the police in Grimsby docks as was the normal practice, echoes of Boar's death many years before. Later in the same year Susan and Peter married it was both a happy and sad occasion Susan had so missed her father he got on so well with Peter and would have been extremely happy by the news of her marriage to Peter. By 1901 Peter and Susan had moved to a nice house in Sculcoates Hessle in Rugby Street. Susan was also by now very heavily pregnant she was due to have their first child at any time. Peter had taken on work as a Coal Heaver with much better pay and by god the pair needed every extra penny that they could get. The work had entailed working on ships, he wasn't a crew member he worked loading the coal into the massive coal bunkers on the ships, having to heave the coal into the huge coal bunkers for the stokers to feed the coal into the hungry boilers it was a very dirty and unenviable job. The heavers worked below decks and in the suffocating hot engine rooms it was a very hot stifling and filthy working environment the coal dust would coat the lungs in thick black dust. Times were very hard and Peter and Susan had eventually taken on a lodger to help ends meet. The lodger was a seaman from Liverpool he would tell Peter so many exaggerated stories about Liverpool and its port. He had told Peter there was so much work to offer a skilled tradesman such as himself. The city's population had grown to 600,85 thousand what the sailor hadn't told Peter was most of the population were extremely poor and many of the population had been forced out of Ireland so had added to the population of Liverpool at the time there was very little housing to accommodate the influx of people. In Grimsby during 1901 there had been a mass strike within the Grimsby docks. It had lasted for fourteen weeks and the dock workers had subsequently been locked out of the docks by the owners without any work the Docker's would not get paid. The dock workers and fishermen had walked en masse towards the docks and began to congregate around the main dock gates. The towns magistrates had requested assistance from the Sheffield elders for more police to help assist the Grimsby police force to put the strike down. An extra 80 policemen had been drafted to persuade the strikers to move on and for the police to disperse the large crowds. On another occasion, the strikers had moved along Cleethorpes road which was very close to Stirling street Susan had heard a commotion and had wandered onto Cleethorpes street as she did so she could see a large crowd of townspeople who were following a squad of policemen and they were marching towards the main dockyard. As the crowd approached Fish Clock road some of the fishermen and other strikers began to hurl stones and rocks towards the police. It was at this point an order had been issued by the police and they had ordered the strikers to clear the streets immediately or they would suffer the consequences. The dock owners had demanded the police to move the hooligans on their way and to arrest any of the trouble makers and more especially the organisers of the strike. The crowd of onlookers had watched from a safe distance and far away from the police lines but for some unknown reason the police had begun to charge the crowd of onlookers and not the striking mob. The Grimsby police had gone after the striking dock workers but unfortunately it had been the Sheffield police who mistakenly charged the onlookers and with such disastrous results, they had crashed headlong into the innocent crowd of bystanders with such force women and children had fallen on top of one another and some of them had been belted with police truncheons for their troubles and there hadn't been any mercy shown by the police blood had been spilt and it covered the cobbles many women and children were crying and those who had been hit were screaming out for help and some of the strikers turned back and began to pull the police off the people who were by now sprawled on the ground some people were also taking such a fierce beating by the police officers with such relish it was an awful scene. The local magistrate had clambered on board the flatbed of a lorry parked close by and began to read the riot act to the crowd, who were by now running amok and smashing crates and there was some looting. There was a cacophony of sounds that added to the commotion of the policemen charging at the crowd and the people in the crowd shouting and screaming and the mixer of sounds were ringing in the air no one could hear what the magistrate had been trying to convey or the severity of the riot act. The following day a contingent of the Manchester mounted police arrived at the docks and they rode along the dock road to display a physical show of strength it also provided a high visible presence within the docks. Luckily there hadn't been a repeat of the previous day's events or further violence. The presence, of the mounted police did much more to help quell the violence of the previous day than having the police charging the crowds with truncheons drawn and being brutal towards the crowds. A policeman riding on a horse can put the fear of god into a rowdy mob the Manchester mounted police were used to dealing with violent crowds. Grimsby in 1901 was a sprawling unsanitary slum and it was in this environment and with the docks strike having suddenly fizzing out that Susan had given birth to her first son Rodmond Frederick Peterson. It was during this uncertain period Peter had decided to take a momentous decision and to move to Hull and far away from Grimsby and the potential for more strikes and the recent industrial unrest subsequently after the strikes had ended no one had been guaranteed work and those workers who had needed to get back to work in the docks had to agree to some new working practices the dock owners had demanded of all the men who had been involved in the strike and they had to sign the new contracts and if they didn't they would never be employed by the owners it was a very stark choice and it was nothing but a form of blackmail. Peter and Susan had a new commitment with the birth of Rodmond, Frederick. Peter had found new work but once again it was as a coal heaver within the Hull docks. The work was very labour intensive having to load flat bottom boats (a type of barge) with coal until five or six barges were full of coal the barges would have to be pulled along by a tug and moored next to the steam ships requiring the coal Peter and his fellow coal heavers would have to load large sacks of coal then they were winched aboard the steam ships these ships would then ply their trade or cargo to the very far ends of the British Empire. Peter took the work as it paid well, better than in the Grimsby Docks, he needed the extra pay because of the recent birth of Rodmond and he was used to the work. A coal heavers trade was a very tough one as many could not carry on with the extreme manual work because as soon as they had hit their forties it was when their bodies had been broken because of the many injuries they picked up having worked as a coal heaver and over the many years their lungs would have coal dust slowly filling their lungs and some of the men would often spew a black tar substance from deep within their lungs it was such a dreadful sight. They weren't the highest paid within the Hull Docks but even so they were far better paid than most of the other manual workers working in the docks the owners of the companies were having to supply coal to the steamships and the ships had a very tight time frame to adhere to and they had to ensure the ships were quickly supplied with coal and then they had to turn the ships around and out of the quayside it would enable the ships following to berth and to make sure that the ships coal bunkers were full of coal the process would be repeated day after day and during the night as there was no slowing down and Peter had hated the night shifts as it was far more dangerous to work under the artificial lighting. The money had helped Peter to provide for Susan and young Rodmond the baby had a middle name it was

25

Frederick the family name was "Freddie" or sometimes Fred. The family had recently moved into another house it was a nice clean rental house and it was situated close to the docks. Life was still a struggle for the family and Peter had to take whatever work that came his way as beggars cannot be choosers. At the time, if he had a choice of work he would have liked to have work on a fishing vessel. Britain was in such a state of flux as the nation's longest reigning monarch. Queen Victoria had been taken seriously ill in the January of the same year 1901 and by the 22nd of January 1901 the Queen passed away. She was 81 and had served as monarch for almost 64 years. Many ordinary Britain's had never known of any other monarch. Prince Albert Edward, The Prince of Wales had succeeded as King Edward VII he was Queen Victoria's eldest son. Queen Victoria's funeral had taken place at Windsor Castle in the February and the Nation was in a period of mourning. When Fred was 12 Peter had decided to move his young family to Liverpool for better opportunities? but Fred did not wish to move as he had left school and he was already earning a wage a decision was made it was for him to remain with his grandmother Mary, she was Susan's mother the reason behind the decision was Peter and Susan against all hope had thought he would soon become bored with staying with his gran and would soon want to move to and join his parents. Two years later and Fred was still living with his grandmother and Susan had given birth to another son Edwin but sadly there had been massive complications during his birth Susan had a very rough and a very uncomfortable and an extremely difficult childbirth baby Edwin had suffered from a severe lack of oxygen to his brain during the birth. Susan was fraught with anxiety regarding the baby's health unfortunately there hadn't been a doctor to assist with the delivery it had been a local midwife well at least she had claimed that she was a midwife Peter had paid her a substantial amount of money for her to assist Susan during the birth of little Edwin. It hadn't only been a lack of oxygen that would cause so many medical problems and during his first few months of life he seemed to have developed even more medical problems and this time it was with his limbs, his arms would suddenly go into spasm and he would suffer convulsions added to everything else he couldn't stand up on his own without some assistance. Susan had taken him to one of the main children's hospitals in Liverpool the doctors at the hospital had diagnosed him with Hydrocephalus and spastic Paraplegia it is a very rare disorder it is where parts of the body develop spasticity and various weakness to the limbs the main feature of the disease is it can be progressive and would eventually cause spasticity to the lower limbs. The limbs are an invalid disorder and it is sometimes inherited. The news was yet another massive bombshell to hit the family and at the time there wasn't any state help and it was up to the family to support Edwin to get by as best they could it was a very difficult time for everyone. Susan blamed herself for Edwin's condition and Peter had tried his very best to console her. The authorities had informed them it could be arranged for Edwin to be consigned to a "special" hospital if they so wished. They had made it sound as though the baby was just an object and not a person they had been a little cold towards the family both Susan and Peter had refused to send him to any institution they had been disgusted and very hurt by such a suggestion by the doctors. They loved baby Edwin and they were under no illusions they knew that things would be very difficult trying to bring him up but as far as possible he would have his loving family around him. There were no special foods or facilities to help Edwin and to make his life that bit more comfortable. Over time Peter was able to find a much better paid job still within the docks and he was employed as a fisherman as his fisherman's apprentice documents were still valid and up to date he didn't own his own boat so he had managed to get a job as the second mate onboard a large fishing vessel which was based and registered in Liverpool the skipper would push the boat and the crew to the very limits of endurance especially when the skipper had fished in the Irish Sea and if the fish were scarce in the designated fishing areas he would fish much further and deeper into the North Atlantic and when the skipper carried out this change of tack the boat and the crew were stretched to the very limits of their endurance but on the plus side the pay was extremely good it was better than breathing in coal dust. Susan in the meantime was spending so much of her time trying to make Edwin as comfortable as possible it had been very difficult for her to understand what the Edwin wanted or needed as he wasn't what one would call a normal child with normal needs due to his medical condition as he had so many different wants and he was incapable of communicating. Times were very hard for most people during this time bringing up a baby for Susan it was even harder. The house they were living in was in Wolfe Street Toxteth, it was very close to the Brunswick Docks where the fishing vessel Peter worked on would moor up. The houses had consisted of terraces they were slightly more comfortable they had been used to it was a three up two down with two families sharing the same house. It was slightly cramped especially with the added pressures of having an invalid child it had been very difficult at the best of times. Susan's and Peter's time was taken up with the everyday needs of Edwin as there wasn't any further medical follow ups or any checkups by the hospital after Edwin was born, they were well and truly on their own. At the time, the National Health Service hadn't been in existence the NHS would not be established until 1948 almost 39 years after Edwin's birth. There was one thing the family could give Edwin in bucket loads and it was kindness and gallons of love. Peter had made a kind of go cart with wooden handles and Susan would place plenty of pillows in the go cart/pram wrapping them around Edwin to keep his torso propped upright as his limbs were very weak but his brain was razor sharp the only problem was he was unable to talk or communicate to those around him. Fred had attended school as normal but obviously at the time there weren't any education facilities for poor Edwin. Susan had been educated by her grandparents they were retired Victorian school teachers and she began to set about educating Edwin along very similar lines as she had been taught. School books were not readily available as they are today many schools and parents who taught their children at home would use a small blackboard and chalk to enable them to teach their own children to read and write. Whenever Susan took Edwin outside to visit the various parks in and around Liverpool she would try to teach him about the plants and the many trees within the city parks. He had great difficulty concentrating and would often have a spasm it was only natural due to his many severe medical conditions some people would point and stare at him in utter disgust. Susan had people some of them complete strangers come up to her and would tell her that he should not be seen out in public and of course their awful remarks deeply hurt Susan and she had often thought that in his own way Edwin had understood what had been said about him she had often thought he could sense and felt he was different to other children. Both Peter and Fred were working extremely hard to keep food in the families' bellies and to keep a roof over their heads Fred would often send some money home to his parents from Hull. On another note during the outbreak of The Great War Peter had many an uneducated person telling him to go back to where he had come from. His accent was very broad it had a strong Nordic twang he could speak, read and write in

English more than his co-workers could and it was all thanks to Susan she had taught Peter to read and write English. To the many uneducated people, they thought he spoke with a strong German accent and not a Norse accent they wouldn't know the difference. The first world war had arrived it was such a shock and it was only the start of an era that would change Peter and the family forever. The war would eventually change everyone who was involved and the world would never be the same again. At the time, no one could imagine the devastation that the war would inflict on many millions of people and over time Peter's accent would cause him even more problems he was suddenly taken off the fishing boat without any explanation he was paid off. He had moved to a lowly paid job and he eventually became a lighter man within the Herculaneum docks. Young Fred had never been an academic and he had left school at the age of 12 the family could not afford to have Fred out of work for a long time it had become an uphill struggle for the family having to look after Edwin. Fred was still living over in Hull at his grandmother's house he had worked on various fishing vessels out in the North Sea and had wanted to make his own way in life. Fred had lied about his age and was taken on by an old and bold skipper he hadn't checked his date of birth and at the break out of war many young men had volunteered for the Royal Navy as Hull was crawling with fishermen it was a great recruiting area for the Royal Navy. In June 1915 as the Germans began to launch the infamous Zeppelins bombing raids on Hull. At the time to the residents it had been like being attacked by spacemen from the moon it was the scariest thing that anyone had ever experienced. The zeppelin was a type of rigid airship and the first air raids on Hull had taken place between the 5th and the 6th of June 1915. Many commercial buildings and some homes had been destroyed and many more homes had been severely damaged during the raids most of the raids had been aimed at the docks area. But inevitably some of bombs had hit the many overcrowded back to back housing very close to the dock area. At the time of the raids the use of air borne bombing was still in its infancy it hadn't been a precise art. Hull had its own form of air raid warning system it was called buzzes and they were huge steam driven whistles two of the larger of the buzzes had been nicknamed "big lizzie" and the "hull mail" the sounds of the buzzes must have seemed very alien to the population. On the fateful day of the fifth of June 1915 Zeppelin L.9 attacked the Hull docks area the raid had lasted for almost thirty minutes' and many of the bombs and incendiary munitions had hit Campbell, Coltman, Constable, Easter, Porter, Queens, South Parade Walker Street and Blanket Row. During the raids, a large bomb had hit the Humber Docks area the bombs had rained down hitting a merchant ship and caused a significant amount of damage. The Holy Trinity Church was hit during the same raid it had caused £100,000 worth of damage. The raid had sadly killed 24 people and had injured a further 40 innocent people. The early morning sky had looked like a horrifying scene from the future as a huge cigar shaped vessel had been caught in the bright lights of several of the search lights. At the beginning of the war there had only a rudimental anti-aircraft system. To the locals the sight of the Zeppelin's in the sky had looked so surreal and at the time no one had ever seen anything like it before mechanised flying terror high in the sky's above mainland Great Britain it was the start of things that were to come. It was also the background to the buildup of resentment and hatred towards those of Germanic heritage living in the United Kingdom it was also why Peter was starting to find it very uncomfortable living in England at the time. Later that very same week as the air raids there had been several riots in Hull and the rioters had only targeted German sounding properties and shops. On the fifth of March 1916 Zeppelins L.11 and L.14 attacked Hull for almost an hour once again they had randomly dropped their cache of bombs and many incendiary devices. Throughout 1916 and up until 1919 Hull had been frequently bombed by the Zeppelins. During the raids Fred had been living in Hull and was working in the docks area he had by now left the fishing fleet and was working as a coal heaver, just like his father, when once again the German's had unleashed the mighty Zeppelin's on the unsuspecting people of Britain. The Zeppelins had also begun to bomb London and killing scores of people in the city Zeppelins had soon became the vehicle of choice for the Germans and had used the Zeppelin's to try and undermine the British war effort and the people's morale living on the home front. Fred's Grandmother Mary had thought that it was becoming far too dangerous for him to remain living in Hull she had sat him down and explained to him of her fears for his safety and how it was becoming far too dangerous for him to stay in Hull with the frequent bombing raids she had told him that it was now time for him to move to his parent's home in Liverpool reluctantly Fred agreed and travelled to his parent's home in Liverpool. The raids were to have disastrous consequences for the family. Peter and his mum Sarah were by now well settled in Liverpool his father was currently working as a lighterman at the number three Dock within the larger Herculaneum inner dock the docks were very close to where the family was living. Each morning Peter had looked forward to going to work and he had a very good work contract and he had been signed up for full time work it was at a time when many dock workers had to queue daily for work and if they were very lucky they would be offered some work the work would only be for a day or perhaps if they were lucky two days but no more. Peter's haversack contained his lunch and a tiny amount of loose tea with which Susan had wrapped in some old newspaper and a tiny amount of sugar including a small bottle of milk. One morning as Peter approached the dock gates he had observed the daily queue of men waiting to see if they would gain employment. Some of the men had hissed and spat at Peter as he walked past the line of men he had also heard someone mutter "fucking foreigner his bloody lot are killing our lads over in France and bombing our city's what the fuck is he still doing still here"? Peter would face the same abuse on an almost daily basis he had hated walking past the queues of men he never told Susan of the abuse he would suffer on an almost daily basis, he had wanted to keep what was happening at work in the workplace and not to bring the realities of what he put up with into his peaceful and tranquil home he had thought to himself what Susan didn't know it would not hurt her, or so he thought. The war was in its second year and there was ever more resentment shown towards "foreign" people in the city. Things would eventually come to a head when on the 7th of May 1915 with the sinking of the passenger liner RMS Lusitania off the coast of Ireland the ship had been sunk by a German Submarine the U20 the ship went down with the loss of 1,198 passengers and crew 761 passengers and crew survived. The ship had been built in Liverpool many of the crew were from the Liverpool area and from the close-knit Irish Community. Later the same year there was an outbreak of extreme violence it had been meted out to so called "foreigners" within the city many German owned shops which bore German names were attacked by the baying crowds and many of the shop windows had been smashed and the goods inside were looted some shops were then firebombed. There were so many more acts of violence meted out to so many innocent people. Peter was treading a very fine line as many of the men working at the dock yard knew he was a foreigner the more educated of the work force knew Peter had been born in the Faroe Islands and not Germany and they had also understood the Islands were part of Denmark and not part of Germany the Faroe Islands are still part of the Danish commonwealth of countries including Greenland. The uneducated person didn't have a clue to where the Faroe Islands where or even where Denmark was in the world. To them Peter was just another bloody dirty Foreigner and was probably working for Germany as a spy. Hatred was running very high more so after the sinking of the passenger liner the Lusitania some people had wanted to take revenge on anyone they had suspected of being German the mob in Liverpool began to turn on anyone who they had thought was German and sometimes it didn't matter who you were or where you came from they would mete out their own form of justice come what may. On occasions a British warship ship would be seen limping into the Herculaneum docks having been hit by cannon fire from a German warship and the battered ships would limp into the docks either having been towed to the dock or if it could manage it under its own power many of the ships that had been hit would have huge canvass sheeting covering any damage at the time it had been deemed by the War Office that it would be bad for the morale of the British public if they saw the damage inflicted on any British shipping be it ships of the Merchant Navy or the Royal Navy it hadn't been something the government of the day wanted advertising. Peter was small of stature and he was very muscular he could look after himself as he was very handy with his fists he would sometimes take part in illegal boxing tournaments within the dock area for some extra money, after many years working on the fishing fleets had made him very tough indeed. He was far more worried about any reprisals which might be carried out on his family. One fateful day the cheerful Peter hadn't returned home after completing his night shift down at the docks. That evening Susan was frantic with worry and she had sent Fred out into the cold dark night to search for his dad at the Herculaneum docks it was the docks his father had been working in as a lighterman. When he arrived at the docks the huge gates at the dockyard had been locked and he could just see through gaps in the gates he could just make out in the distance a night watchman he was sat around a brazier he was obviously attempting to warm up during the very cold evening. Fred tried his very best to catch the watchman's attention and he began to shout at the man but alas his cries had fallen on deaf ears he resorted to throwing stones over the gates he could see that the night watchman was beginning to get annoyed and even more so when a stone hit him on his arm Fred had at last got the man's attention he could see the watchman walking towards the dock gates the man looked very angry indeed. He began to shout at Fred "what the fuck do you think you are bloody doing arse hole now what do you bloody want? Fred didn't get a chance to answer him back as the man shouted "now fuck off if you know what's good for you and if you don't bugger off and fast I'll come over there and give you a bloody thick ear" Fred had managed to calm him down just long enough to be able to ask him if he had seen his dad Mr Peter Peterson he had quickly described what his dad did in the docks and described what he looked like the watchman seemed to know Peter he told Fred no one was left in the dockyard apart from those authorised to be in the docks at night. Fred had reluctantly turned around and had left and he felt bitterly disappointed that he hadn't found his dad. On the way home, he had sneaked into one or two of the local pubs the Herculaneum Bridge Hotel and the Trafalgar on the corner of Regent Road and he had run quickly into each of the pubs he had desperately wanted to see if his dad was in any of the pubs and maybe having a sneaky couple of pints before returning home. It would have been highly unusual if he had been drinking in the pubs Fred had thought to himself if he quickly scurried around inside the pubs no one would be able to grab hold of him to give him a thick ear for having entered the pubs. As it was no one caught him as most of the drinkers were very merry and far too slow to grab him and yes, he had been sworn at and told in no uncertain terms to leave the pub. During this time Pubs weren't a place for wives or girlfriends they were a no go places for children many of the pubs were seen as havens for the working man to wind down after work and they were a place where they could relax and blot out the harsh conditions of the work place and later in the same year new licensing rules would soon come into effect because many of the working men would spend most of their money in the pubs and the family would end up suffering the consequences of not having any money to live on life was a dreary tread mill of an existence. On the way home Fred decided to try one more pub it was on his route home and he had already scoured many pubs so one more wouldn't hurt and he soon found himself walking along Mill Street and had managed to get himself inside The Derby Arms (Dead Man) pub and once again he ran into the pub and once again he felt ever so disappointed his dad was nowhere to be seen Fred had left the pub in such a hurry as he knew his mum would be getting worried about his whereabouts and she would be thinking something may have happened to him she currently had enough to be worrying about without him adding to her woes. When he eventually arrived home his mum was almost hysterical at the news Fred had brought back with him as he had explained to her that his dad was nowhere to be seen in the vicinity Susan knew it wasn't like Peter to not come straight home after work the situation was extremely worrying. Susan was so concerned because of the continued hostilities and anger growing in the country towards any person of German descent and Liverpool was no exception. Susan had placed Edwin into his adapted pram and told Fred to go and put his jacket back on as they were all about to go out onto the streets to look for Peter. Susan and Fred trudged along the cobbled streets he was pushing his brother along the cobbles sat in his makeshift pram to the local police station. When they arrived at the station Edwin began to play up he could sense there was something so very wrong and he began to make noises some very ignorant people who didn't know the family were staring and pointing towards Edwin sitting in his makeshift pram some people had made some very extremely distained and rude remarks towards Susan such things like "He should not be allowed out onto the streets looking like that you should be ashamed of yourself" Susan was a very strong character and by god over the years she had needed to be and had ignored the distasteful remarks. Inside the police station there were a few prostitutes and many dregs of humanity some were heard to say, "it's that boy again" Susan asked Fred to sit down and to keep an eye on Edwin for her and she approached the desk Sergeant he was managing the front of the very busy Police station. The sergeant knew of the Peterson family very well he was also aware of the current political feelings and the anger building up within the country towards those of German origin the growing resentment towards most foreigners within the city. The sergeants name was Sergeant Jones he was an old and bold policeman he had said, "Ah Mrs Peterson and what can I do for you tonight"? Susan explained about how Peter had gone missing and her alarm bells had sounded especially when he hadn't returned home from work. Sergeant Jones wrote down some notes down into his pocket book and after a few minutes he told Susan to go home and he would carry out some enquiries regarding her husband's sudden disappearance but needed to be aware the cogs of justice would turn very slowly. The country was at war and the police had many other priorities. Policing was so very different to those during peace time at the time they had a lot more important matters on their hands rather than finding an errant husband. Reluctantly Susan and the boys left the police station and began to walk back to their cold and damp flat Susan had so many things going through her mind they all centred around Peter and what had happened to him, he was a family man and would never think of squandering his wages on drink or gambling he was very happy with his lot and with his work like everyone at the time the working conditions could have been a little bit better but it was just the sign of the times and beggars can't be choosers as work paid well. Back at the Police Station Sergeant Jones instructed his bobbies before they went out on patrol to keep an eye out for Peter Peterson or anyone that fitted his description he also pointed out the obvious he might have gone out drinking and for the bobbies to keep their eyes peeled particularly at chucking out time from the various ale houses. When Susan and the children had arrived back at the family's room it looked so drab there was paint peeling from the walls the room only had one main bed for Susan and Peter and there was a bunk bed for Fred and Edwin privacy had only consisted of a thread bare curtain it was draped over some string to hide the bunk bed away from the main room. There was also a trickle of water running down a wall. The room wasn't much but for Susan and Peter it had been better than nothing. She had made a mug of tea for herself and the boys and she was fretting with worry just then Fred spoke up "mam please don't worry dad will come back, you'll see? Susan broke down and sobbed uncontrollably and replied, "it is so very kind of you to say so son but I don't think your dad will ever return home your because your dad has never done this sort of thing before". That night the Peterson household had a very disturbed sleep and of course

Edwin was oblivious to everything which was going on around him and that night he had been the only one who had managed to have a blissful night's sleep. Susan and Fred had woken up very early the following morning and at breakfast Susan said to Fred "I suppose no news is good news isn't it son? if the police had found your dad last night they would have told me by now surely?". Fred wasn't sure if his mum had believed what she had said. Once again Susan dragged the children around to the local Police station to check if there had been any news regarding Peter's disappearance. The night shift sergeant had left the station and instead standing at the front counter was a sergeant who Susan never seen before. The sergeant was an ex-boxer and anyone looking at him could see he had been a boxer just by the shape of his broken and very flat nose and he had old scars covering his lips. On the counter, there was a small block of wood with his name inscribed on it "Sergeant O'Neill. When she saw his name, she had recognised it but only by his reputation as a no-nonsense type of policeman. Susan had once again explained why she was visiting the police station aa she had wanted to check if her husband Peter had been found yet? Sergeant O'Neill immediately ordered her not ask any more questions he told her to remain exactly where she was and not to move he left the counter area and walked towards the rear of the Police Station Susan stood on her tip toes to see where he had disappeared to and she could just make out some offices towards the rear of the station. When he returned the Station, Inspector was with him the look on their faces was very stern and serious. As soon as Susan saw the expressions on their faces she knew immediately something was seriously wrong and suddenly she had let out a primitive animal sounding wail and she cried out "Oh no you have found him, haven't you?" Fred looked over towards his mum and said "what do you mean mum? Have they arrested dad?" Susan replied, "no son your dad is dead sweetheart" Susan was shaking uncontrollably and by now she had slumped onto a bench crying her tears were streaming down her face. Fred had begun to cry and his tears were cascading uncontrollably down his face he was heaving as he was trying to be strong unsuccessfully to control his emotions. At that moment Susan's world had collapsed around her and as she sat in the foreboding police station her life would never be the same again. The Inspector invited Susan to step into his office Fred was told to stay at the front of the police station and look after Edwin even the Inspector had felt slightly uncomfortable with an invalid child in his police station there was a lot prejudice in society at the time. Edwin hadn't a clue as to what was going on around him he lived in a world of his own. He had seemed to understand there was something very wrong with his brother he was unable to console him and for Edwin his feelings and his inability to communicate with his brother was making him feel very frustrated and was starting to have one of his "turns". Once inside the Inspectors office Susan was invited to sit down she was offered a cup of tea she accepted the offer as her throat was very dry. It was at this point the Inspector had informed Susan everything he knew about Peter's disappearance. He told Susan to prepare herself for some bad news Peter's body was eventually found floating in No3 Dock it was a smaller dock within a much larger dock known as Herculaneum dock. It was the same place where Peter had been working during his night shift. It had been the Police's day shift who had first entered the dock area. It had been first thing in the morning and they had found Peter's body floating face down in the polluted water of No3 dock. The Inspector went on to explain there would have to be a post mortem carried out on his body because of the circumstances surrounding his death. Susan had wanted to know why there was a need for a post mortem or an autopsy if it had only been a drowning accident. The Inspector went on to explain that he hadn't been totally convinced it had been a case of an accidental drowning he continued to explain as best he could. He had informed the city coroner surrounding his concerns and his suspicions surrounding Peter's unfortunate death. It was at this point the penny had suddenly dropped and she had begun to realise that her beloved Peter might have been murdered it hadn't been an accident she said, "oh my poor Peter what had he ever done to deserve such a horrible death" she had realised the Police were thinking he had been murdered while he was at work and had been too much for her to take on board she was in deep shock at the news. She had thought "oh my poor Peter killed and left in the filthy cold dock water and left all on his own just like a piece of discarded rubbish to be tossed away" after some thought Susan asked, "where is he now?". She had begun to regain her composure and had pulled herself together and had begun to think straight she said, "I want to be with him" The inspector replied, "Your husband's body is currently at the city mortuary I must warn you he has suffered some very severe injuries to the back of his head" Peters body had been taken to the local coroner's office at the city mortuary. She had left the police station and had taken the boys to a neighbour's house as she hadn't wanted to take Fred to see his father's body besides he was only fourteen he was far too young to be looking at corpses especially his fathers. It was late morning the family had been at the police station for quite a few hours. Susan eventually arrived at the coroner's office where she was shown into a very cold room it was the examination room it was to the rear of the coroners building. Peter had been lain out on a cold metal table and his body had been covered with a white sheet. He looked so peaceful and at rest Susan bent over his face and kissed his forehead suddenly she had reeled back in horror as his skin had felt so very cold it was very clammy to the touch on her lips. The last time she had kissed Peter had been the previous morning when he had left home for work and he had been happily whistling on his way to do a day's work. As she looked down at Peter's skin it had looked very pale and his lips had turned a purply blue colour. She had gasped in horror as she saw the back of Peters head it was obvious to everyone in the room he had been dealt a severe blow to the rear of his head there was some very thick and heavy stitching to the back of his head. It had been where the pathologist had entered the rear of Peter's skull for him to get access and to examine the cause of his violent death. The coroner took Susan into his warm office she looked back towards where Peter was laid out on the metal table she knew that it would be the very last time she would ever see him again she was inconsolable with grief. The coroner had begun to explain to Susan as to why he hadn't been happy surrounding the circumstances of Peter's death. Susan responded "why? I thought he had accidently drowned and might have smashed his head against something hard in the water? it had been all too obvious to the coroner it hadn't been an accident and he told her in his opinion Peter had been attacked from behind Susan had heard his words but she had blanked out any thoughts of her poor Peter having been murdered. The coroner broke her train of thought all she had taken in were the words "because he was found floating in the dock and with massive damage to the back of the head" the coroner continued to explain about the need for a coroner's inquest and that it would be held at the coroner's court within the week. At the same time as Susan was sat in the coroner's office Fred had left the neighbour's house with his brother in tow he was sat in the dingy room knowing his dad was dead and he would never again walk through the door ever again it seemed so final and the news had hit him very hard he had managed to get Edwin onto the bottom bunk bed as he was unable to talk when he became over excited he would just mumble and his eyes would become larger and would begin to bulge in their sockets he would flail with his arms he was very strong. Fred stroked his head as it would normally calm him down and would make him so much easier to handle. It wasn't too long before his brother had dropped off to sleep and he knew his brother was aware something was wrong. While Fred waited for his mum to return from the coroner's office he began to pace up and down he was so scared and he had feared about what the future would hold for the family as his dad had been the main bread winner and they could only just afford the little they had. He knew if the family couldn't afford to pay the rent they would be thrown out onto the street penniless. Susan had returned home and she was crying she was extremely distraught she thought is this all we are worth is this the total of what Peter and I have managed to provide for our children she looked around the room and saw Edwin was fast asleep she could see Fred was sat on one of the three rickety chairs around an old dirty kitchen table as it was the only furniture in the room. He looked up at his mum and spoke "Its dad isn't it mam?" she replied, "yes son I am afraid it is your dad" he suddenly burst out crying and said, "oh mam what is going to happen to us now", she sobbed "I really don't know sweetheart, I just don't know". She surveyed the room she had two children a 14 year old boy and a severely handicapped 12 year old boy both of whom would be dependent on her as the sole bread winner. At this point in her life she did not know what the future would hold for any of them. It was soon time for the coroner's inquest Susan was in attendance including the Police and there were various dock workers and the dockyard management they were attending as witnesses and there were members of the press and a few members of the public. The coroner's initial findings regarding the suspicious circumstances surrounding the death of Peter Peterson had leant towards the evidence that he had been murdered by person or persons unknown. In his opinion, it had been found beyond any doubt it had been a case of murder and not an accidental death. During 1915 it had been such a divisive time in the country. As mentioned Liverpool at the time had recently seen many attacks on Germans and attacks on second generation Germans and people with German names including their property many properties had been attacked and severely damaged and occasionally they had been deliberately fire bombed it was a dreadful time. It was suspected even though Peter wasn't German he had been killed by one or more persons and had been attacked within the dock where he had been working he had been hit on the back of the head with a blunt instrument Peter's body was disposed of in the water of No3 dock and it had been established beyond any doubt when he had been thrown into the water he was still alive the autopsy had confirmed he was alive due to the fact that his lungs were full of water hence the coroner had recorded in his report beyond any doubt he was still alive when he had entered the water. When Susan had heard the coroners evidence she had cried out she had tried desperately to regain her composure by now the court room was in deadly silence. The coroners court had heard the evidence submitted by the police and they had confirmed he had been killed within the docks and after exhaustive enquiries they could not identify who the perpetrator or preparators were as the Dockers had closed ranks and no one was going to provide any information which might have helped to solve Peter's murder. The police had been frustrated at every turn during their investigations it had been the local Police force who had been informed of a body floating in the docks and when the police eventually recovered the body they could see that the back of Peter's head had been caved in by a blunt instrument and it had been very obvious the instrument could have been picked up from around the dockside as there was plenty of wood and other debris any one of the items laying around could have so easily been used to hit Peter over the back of the head. The Pathologist and the coroner having examined the body ascertained it had been in the water for several hours and most certainly the body had lain in the water overnight. They had found it incredulous that no one working in the dock hadn't noticed Peter's body floating in the dock until the next morning. The coroner carried on with his evidence and described the wound to the back of the head initially the pathologist thought there was a very slight possibility Peter may have slipped and banged his head on something on the dockside and he had eventually fell into the water and drowned. On further investigation, the pathologist ascertained beyond any reasonable doubt the wound could only have been caused by someone hitting him from behind and in his conclusion, was the same as the coroners in that Peter had been killed by person or persons unknown. The court proceedings had continued for another week with the conclusion the killers or killer beyond any doubt had deliberately killed him and whoever the person or persons were never apprehended. The police had their suspicions regarding to who the killers might have been and the same people had worked within the same dock as Peter and they had more than likely known him and he had possibly known who his killers were. The murder case was left on Police files as unresolved. At this point in Susan's life she had been left destitute the landlord had soon turfed the family out of their room. Susan, Fred and Edwin were now out on the street with nowhere to go. Luckily enough within the city Peter had some family members who were from the Faroe Islands and as soon as they had heard about Peter's demise and the plight of Susan and the children they had taken the family in for a short period of time so that Susan could find somewhere else to live. Susan didn't have the means to give Peter a decent burial but the various Docker's organisations and the docks company who employed him had provided the funds for Peter to have a decent funeral and a burial in St James's cemetery close to the Liverpool Anglican Cathedral. Susan had taken on work in the city's main bakery the work had been shift work Fred would look after Edwin during the period Susan was working the night shift. At the same time, she was working at the bakery there was a nice man he was a foreman and his name was Henry they had got on very well so well that they had met up after a shift and Susan had told him all about Peter and more importantly about Edwin and his medical situation. One day Susan had felt confident enough and had invited Henry back to her home it had been a massive leap of faith on Susan's part she had introduced him to Fred and Edwin. At first it had been a bit of a shock for him when he saw Edwin as he hadn't fully understood or even imagined the severity of Edwin's medical condition. After a few months of seeing Susan he soon got used to Edwin's condition and he would often take him out for walks pushing him around the parks in his homemade wheel chair. Henry was ten years older than Susan he was very wise he had recently retired from serving in the Army. He had never married and some would say he had married the Army he had joined the Army as a boy soldier. He would regale Fred with stories of his Army service this had made him even more determined to "join up". Henry had one or two scars from his service with the Army in 1902 he had been serving with the 4th Battalion the Kings Liverpool Regiment it was during the second Boer war in South Africa and he had served in the Cape Colony and The Orange Free state and after his service in South

Africa he had been awarded the Kings South African Medal with two bars. Fred would often sit listening to him as he spoke about his Army service Edwin would also be wheeled into the room and he would also listen to Henry's stories he would become very excited by his tall stories. Henry was fully aware of the boy's father's murder he was also very aware of Fred's simmering anger. Henry was very happy with Susan as she was very loving she was also a very caring person it had got to the point when Henry had plucked up the courage to propose to her it was now 1918. After Henry had proposed to Susan she had dearly wanted to move back to the Hull area as Liverpool had held so many bad memories for her and she remembered the torment caused by her late husband's death she had only remained in the city because of the past. Each week she would visit his grave to lay fresh flowers on his grave. She had always felt she had owed it to his memory. Henry had tried many times to try and explain to her that life must move on she needed to breathe and live her life again; Peter's memories would always be with her no matter what or wherever she was living. Henry was a practical person and he was very realistic and he had seen enough of life to know life was for the moment and it had to be grabbed with both hands to enable her to start to live life to the full. Henry had been receiving a small pension on retirement from the Army and he was receiving a smaller pension resulting from the many wounds he had received during his service in South Africa. 1919 would turn out to be a very busy year for Susan as it would be the same year she would marry Henry it was also the same year her son Fred had managed to join the Army after his first attempt had failed. Fred was still feeling very angry about what had happened to his dad and in his mind, he had been murdered because of his place of birth even though he hadn't been born in Germany or even spoke German. At the time it was how many in the country were reacting to what had happened during The Great War and all the misery it had brought to the people of Great Britain the country was suffering as were so many millions of people who had suffered the consequences of the great war a generation had been killed or maimed on the front in France and their deaths would have ramifications for generations to come it had affected the psyche of the British people he had felt the same about the death of his dad. Susan would find things very difficult as Peter had been the main bread winner and Edwin being severely handicapped. Edwin was by now so much older and he was becoming a little bit of a handful as he had become so much stronger he would sometimes lash out of pure frustration his mind was sharp as a button and extremely alert even though he had brain damage. His body had degenerated but not his strength but he was extremely strong his body didn't function like a normal healthy person and he couldn't walk his arms and hands were unable to operate properly. The anger felt by Fred had gradually ate away inside and he wanted to prove to others that his family were very loyal towards Britain and he had felt he wanted to take revenge on the nation he had blamed for causing the death of his dad. In fact, it had been down to the individuals who had murdered his father and not the German people it was just how he had viewed the situation that his family had found themselves in. It was early 1917 and Fred was by now approaching 16 he had looked so much younger than 16. Henry was worried about Fred as he was far too young to join the Army. Susan and Henry had decided once they were married, they would move to Hull Fred had already decided to move back to Hull ahead of his mother he had moved back to his grandmother's house. Susan had realised that he was growing up fast and had wanted to lead his own life so Fred had moved back to Hull he still had a strong desire to join the Army.

Chapter 3 – Marriage and Ireland

At the time Lord Kitchener was the secretary of state for the Army and he needed even more recruits to enter the killing machine, as the Great War had become as it was just like a mince grinder having to be fed more and more men and to then spew out the mangled and broken men thousands of men from all sides had been killed and maimed and yet even more men were required to satisfy the war machine over in France. The nick name given to the fresh recruits was "Kitchener's Army" the recruitment drive encouraged companies, streets and areas to volunteer en masse hence the various names given to the new Battalions "pals' battalions" or in the case of one particular battalion from Grimsby the "Grimsby Chums", it was formed by former schoolboys. Wherever anyone looked in the streets of Britain at the time there were thousands of young men in uniform be it Army or Royal Navy dress no one could escape the uniforms of war. Crowds would gather around anyone of fighting age who was not dressed in a military uniform and would humiliate them for not answering the call of duty for even more men to enlist. To avoid humiliation for those attested and who had not yet joined their regiments an arm band was issued to show the public that they were awaiting their call up papers to join one of the many Regiments. Those who had not enlisted were known as slackers and Fred saw this daily and even though he wasn't old enough to enlist he had trotted off to the recruitment office at Pryme Street and he had felt ten feet tall as he walked into the impressive recruitment building he could see lots of men queuing to do their duty and at the time like all young boys Fred had a rose tinted outlook to wanting to enlist in the

Army and wanting to do his duty for King and country. He would soon buck up his ideas when a corporal who was sitting at a trestle table which was laid out with the Union Jack flag draped over the top of it. The corporal was wearing several medal ribbons including The Queen's Africa medal and the Kings Africa medal and he shouted "Next, come on son stop holding up the queue and don't piss me off I am a very busy person" Fred thought great it's my turn and he stepped up to the table the corporal bellowed "Age" Fred replied "eighteen Sir" The corporal slowly looked up from the papers laid out on the table and replied "Fuck off son, pull the other one it's got bells on it", "your no older than my sisters boy" Fred had somewhat failed to bluff this old and bold soldier, The corporal then barked out "Next, now boy listen to me just piss off this is a man's war now run along to your mummy your bloody time will come soon enough now clear off" Fred reluctantly left the recruiting office past the line of men who were volunteering the line snaked out of the building and down the street. He vowed to join the Army come what may and he swore he wouldn't give up trying. Fred eventually obtained an apprenticeship on a fishing boat working out in the North Sea and over the years he grew into a very strong man the work at sea was long and arduous it would eventually turn him into a much wiser person and nothing much would scare him and he still had a longing to enlist before the war would come to an end. On the twelfth of March 1918 Fred was staying at Sculcoates Avenue in Hull he had been visiting a friend and suddenly without warning it was about one thirty in the morning he was woken by the sounds of bombs exploding close and a few minutes later the buzzer alarms built in and around the Hull area had gone off sounding a warning to the population of Hull of a Zeppelin raid. The buzzer alarm system was a very rudimental early warning system they were a steam driven air raid warning system and one of the buzzers had been nicknamed "Big Lizzie" and the alarms had sounded for five minutes but so many people were still in their beds and still fast asleep some people had simply ignored the warnings of the imminent attack on the city. It was during this environment Fred had met a young lady her name was May they had been seeing one another for a short while and they had formed a very romantic and a somewhat heated relationship the relationship was full of passion. They went on to have a whirlwind romance her parents were very alarmed and concerned that it was far too quick for them to be so romantically involved it was the kind of relationship that only occurred during times of war and when people were living through extreme and very violent times and were trying to make the most of life as it could end in a split second. The Zeppelin attacks had made Fred even more eager to enlist and to serve his country he had realised he was under age to legally volunteer and enlist even though it was a time of great need for more and more volunteers and a lot of the recruitment centres would turn a blind eye to many underage volunteers. In 1918, he had once again found himself stood outside the same Army recruiting office that he had been thrown out of on a previous occasion it was when he had blatantly lied about his age but on this occasion, he did not think any of the same recruiting staff would be manning the office as most of them had probably been killed at some point during fighting for King possibly on the front line in France. It was now fast approaching October 1918 and much of the population had thought surely the war would end soon it just couldn't possibly go into a fifth year it just couldn't possibly continue as it was draining the blood of the nation? No one in the country were thinking the war would end very soon sometime at the end of 1918 once again there was push for ever more manpower to fill the killing fields of France as the cream of the nation's young men were lying dead in a foreign field. Inside the recruitment centre Fred was asked to confirm his age and once again he had lied about his age this time he had kept his fingers crossed for luck. The recruitment sergeant was extremely suspicious of Fred's age he knew Fred was lying but he just couldn't prove it as Fred looked so young and the recruitment sergeant didn't believe what he had just told him. During this period of the war no one knew if the German Zeppelins would launch further attacks on the city. The recruitment sergeant had checked with the officer in charge of the Recruitment office and the Officer walked into the main office and took one look at Fred and told the sergeant he had thought everything was in order and in his opinion, he thought Fred was old enough to join the Army and for the sergeant to get Fred signed up immediately as there was no time to waste. The Officer turned to the sergeant and barked out an order "sergeant get this healthy lad to sign his enlistment papers and to make it snappy and process the lad's relevant paper work". At the time, the people of Hull were in an extremely angry mood and they wanted the government of the day to do everything within its power to stop further bombing of the city and for the government of the day to eradicate Germany's ability to rage war on Great Britain so to that end there had been a further requirement for ever more manpower to boost the Army's strength and to make up for the heavy losses on the frontline in France and to break the stalemate. 1919 was a momentous year for the family and even more so for Susan as she had eventually married in the April to her Henry he was much older than her and in fact he was ten years older than she was. At the time, he was a Reserve fireman and he had been discharged from the Army quite a while ago at the time he was far too old to be called up and to serve in the current war. He would often regale Fred of his adventures during his service in the Army over in South Africa he had fought during the second Boer War he had served in the cape colony and the Orange Free State. As soon as Fred had successfully completed his military training the great war had suddenly come to an end and for the nation there was much to celebrate about and a period of mourning. The end of the great war was the firing gun for the slow and eventual demise of the British Empire. The violence in the world had not come to a sudden end but there was another war on the horizon which would soon rear its ugly head it was a war of independence and it was right on Britain's door step it was the Irish war of independence, Cog adh na Saoirse. As soon as Fred had successfully completed his military training he had joined his regiment it was a cavalry regiment The Royal Hussars in November of 1919 the regiment was based in cavalry barracks Canterbury it was classed as a bit of a cushy posting in the lovely city of Canterbury the Regiment had deserved a break having served throughout the Great War and once the war came to an end the Regiment was part of the Army of occupation in the Rhineland Germany. In Canterbury, the only thing the soldiers had to look forward to was Regimental drill and yet more drill and full ceremonial dress parades the Regiment had supplemented military drill with horsemanship and live firing at the local military ranges. The Regiment had recently and had gallantly served in France during the Great War and had only recently returned from an added 6 month tour as part of the Rhine Army of Occupation in and around Konigshaven many of the Regimental officers who had served at the time thought the duty as occupation forces was very distasteful and to many of them it hadn't seemed right. During the occupation the Regiment had also been based within the Rhine area close to the French border. The Regiment had spent almost four years fighting during the Great war and now it had the dubious pleasure of policing the Rhineland. Fred had joined the Regiment straight from training and as a green raw recruit he was about to join a Regiment which had recently been heavily involved in the horrendous carnage of the Great War. It was going to be a very difficult period for any recruit joining a combat experienced Regiment as the recruits would join a Regiment whose men had witnessed a great deal of death and carnage. At the same time, there was the added problem many of the Regiments "old" soldiers had recently been demobilised from the Army and immediately after the end of hostilities also some as soon as they had completed the Regiments tour of duty as part of the Army of occupation of the Rhine. For Fred life had felt so good as at the time he was engaged to the love of his life May the pair had recently moved into rented rooms in Walcott Street they were living just off Hessle Road in Hull. They had planned to get married sometime in 1922 Fred had thought he might be able to get married in his Regimental dress uniform. Things would soon change for the worse Fred had somehow obtained a very rare "leave pass" from the Regiment and he was able to travel to Hull he would frequently travel to Hull at the weekends provided he dint have any duties to perform. Having a leave pass for a week or two was certainly rare at the time. whilst based in Canterbury he would be issued a leave pass for a week leave only if there weren't any other military engagements that he was involved in. But all of that was about to change in the march of 1920, It was a beautiful and sunny morning and the Regiment's Commanding Officer ordered the Squadron Commanders to form their troops up in Regimental formation on the Regimental Parade Square and at the time Fred was in his squadron office when his sergeant major ,SSM, ordered the clerks to run to the troop lines and to get the men out of the various squadron buildings and to form up on the parade square with their mounts the SSM looked at Fred and shouted "Peterson don't just fucking stand there, I meant you as well you thick sod on your way to the stables tell everyone you see to get on parade do you hear me?" Fred shouted back "yes sir", Fred thought to himself and laughed "that is the only time I can shout back at the sergeant major". A very short time later the whole Regiment was on parade including their mounts. Sometime later the Commanding Officer trotted onto the parade square he was sat astride his own mount he looked resplendent dressed in his ceremonial uniform. He began by addressing the Regiment "Gentlemen I have today received orders from the War Office, the Regiment has received orders to deploy to Ireland on the 22nd of April of this year I want every member of the Regiment including the Regiments equipment to be operationally ready for deployment with mounts before the end of March and all Regimental leave has hereby been cancelled and the Regiment will be training up to the day it will deploy to Ireland he paused do I make myself clear gentlemen?". The Regiment responded in unison "yes sir" apart from Fred who was absolutely gob smacked by the news he suspected there were a lot more soldiers at the same time thinking the same as he was. Fred sat astride his beloved horse "George" and thought "for fuck sake how the bloody hell am I going to tell May about this sodding latest bit of news? the old man has just stopped all bloody leave". On the 16th of March just a few days later after the Commanding Officers address to the Regiment and late one evening Fred had made a foolish decision to jump over a wall at the rear of the camp and as he ran through the streets of Canterbury the sunrise hadn't yet broken through the still darkened skies Fred was taking such a massive risk by going AWOL, Absent without Leave, it was a very serious offence as the Regiment had recently been placed under War Office orders to deploy on operations it was very lucky for Fred that the Regiment hadn't been ordered to deploy to war as

Fred could have been shot for desertion and by a firing squad or he could have been charged for cowardliness. It hadn't been one of Fred's most sensible of ideas that he had ever come up with. The only thing that Fred could think about was getting himself to Hull and to try to explain things to May regarding the situation he currently found himself in. Fred had eventually arrived in Hull only after a couple of days hitch hiking and moving on foot by night May had been expecting Fred as the Royal Military Police had visited her house only the previous day having come around to check to see if Fred had been in contact with her. May had told them she didn't know where Fred was but an hour or so later they returned with a civilian policeman and he had a warrant to search the property to ascertain if Fred was in the house luckily for Fred he was nowhere to be seen. So, when Fred arrived at the house a day later May had heard someone knocking on the rear door and she gingerly opened the door and she was suddenly in a state of shock when she saw that it was indeed Fred who was stood at the door, "oh bloody hell Fred you need to get back to your Regiment and quickly you are in so much trouble" he responded, "I bloody know but I just needed to see you before I left for Ireland". May said "quick get inside before a nosy neighbour dobs you in to the police". Fred sat down at the kitchen table and began to explain about the situation he found himself in and he went on to explain as best he could he didn't know how or when they would be able to get married because of the situation with his Regiment's deployment to Ireland. Fred stayed around the area for a couple of days he was pushing his luck until one day he noticed the Royal Military Police were rounding up a soldier who must have also been Absent Without Leave (AWOL) from his own Regiment. Fred observed how the police were treating him they were roughly man handling him things were beginning to hot up so he had quickly walked home and sat down beside May and he explained to her it would be so much better on himself if he returned to the Regiment and just "handed himself in" to the Regimental Police at the guardroom rather than let the Royal Military Police, RMP, catch him and arrest him as he would most certainly receive a far harsher sentence. It would be so much better on him if he re-joined his Regiment under his own volition and hand himself in to the Regimental Police at the Guardroom he should end up receiving a far lesser sentence just by the fact of voluntarily "handing himself in" he explained to May the Royal Military Police were very close by and it wouldn't be too long before they would come back and search for him during the time he was AWOL he had kept hold of his uniform and it was for a very good reason as if he had destroyed his uniform or had deliberately got rid of it, it could have been construed as desertion and yes he had gone AWOL but only for the sole purpose of seeing May and to try and explain about the situation he had found himself in before he had left for Ireland but he hadn't deserted. Before he had left Hull, he told May he would write as soon as he had been released from the Regimental jail and she had told him if he was ok then it was good enough for her May gave him enough money for the train fare to get him back to Canterbury. Fred finally arrived in Canterbury a day later and he had by this time been AWOL for 21 days he knew he was in a great deal of trouble. As soon as he arrived at Canterbury railway station he had entered the gent's toilets where he changed into his uniform no one would bat an eyelid because there were many soldiers boarding or alighting various trains within the station. He smartly marched himself into Cavalry barracks and immediately into the Regimental Guardroom where the Regimental Police Sergeant was sat at his desk he had to do a double take when he had seen Fred stood in front of him and smartly standing at attention, "bloody hell the prodigal son has bloody decided to honour us with his presence ok sunshine fucking march yourself smartly into cell number 2 and make it bloody snappy". The following morning Fred was on Commanding Officers orders and he was subsequently charged with having gone Absent Without Leave, AWOL. At the time, it was such a serious charge and not to be taken lightly. Fred was right about what he had told May and it was because he had voluntarily surrender himself to his Regiments police he was awarded a much lesser sentence the Commanding Officer had awarded Fred 14 days' imprisonment incarcerated in the Regiments jail at the Regimental guardroom. Normally a Commanding Officer would have awarded 21 days imprisonment it meant that Fred would eventually be released from jail on the 21st of April a day before the Regiment was due to deploy to Ireland. After he had done his "time" he immediately mobilised with the Regiment and in April 1920 the Regiment had found itself deployed on the ground in Ireland. The Regiments main role in Ireland was to counter the dissident activities of Sinn Fein and the Irish Republican Army (IRA). The Regiment had initially been billeted within Curragh camp until the General Officer Commanding Ireland ordered the newly arrived Regiment to deploy to County Clare and by the 24th of April the Regiment had found itself on operations within the county is situated on the western side of Ireland it is made up of the craggy cliffs on the Atlantic coastline it is in contrast with the rolling countryside situated in the middle and the east of the county. Some of the regiments squadrons were based at Ennis where and they would be deployed on many operations. Later in the campaign they were deployed to the many other districts of Ireland. In County Clare, it was a very dangerous place to be based during the unit's time in the county a policeman and a soldier had suddenly disappeared they had been unaccounted for by their colleagues many searches had been carried out to find them and rumours were rife about what had eventually had happened to them. At the time, it had been rumoured they had been executed by a local IRA unit and had then been secretly buried. Fred hadn't liked the sound of the news it was bad enough having to do what they were doing in Ireland and then to be captured by the IRA didn't bode well especially when policemen and soldiers were suddenly disappearing and then having been summarily executed. In the June of 1920 a soldier from a Scottish Regiment had jumped from one of four military trucks that he had been travelling in. The trucks had been travelling in convoy and after the soldier had managed to jump from the moving truck he had soon disappeared into a field of long grass but the convoy had carried on its way the commander hadn't bothered to search for the soldier. It was said the soldier had been courting a local woman and he had absconded from the military convoy with the sole idea of meeting up with the woman it hadn't taken too long for him to be "picked up" by members of the local IRA unit he was subsequently court martialled by members of the hierarchy who ran the local IRA unit and subsequently he was sentenced to death. He was supposedly buried in an unmarked grave his body was never found. At the same time, there were some Scottish Regiments who had a very bad reputation within the local population of County Clare. It was in this volatile environment that Fred's Regiment would be used to scour the countryside and to hinder the movements of all IRA unit's who were operating within the same area and at the same time to gather as much intelligence for the Intelligence branch based at the British Army Headquarters in Dublin it was during the Great War the Regiment had been successfully scattered to many French villages and had also been used by the general staff to scatter the squadrons they were sometimes broken down into much smaller units all the way down to troop level. Once they had arrived in Ireland the Regiment was once again deployed as mounted cavalry it was their traditional mounted cavalry role and they had been used during their deployment as flying columns to counteract the IRA's own use of flying columns they had been used many times in this role and to a great success. The tactics used had helped to hamper the terrorist's ability to operate with impunity within the vast expanse of countryside and it also enabled the Army to counter the activities of Sinn Fein and the Irish Republican Army (IRA). It was in 1920 when the IRA had decided to form its own flying columns and they had consisted of very small groups of insurgents sometimes they were made up to twenty to thirty men and some of the guerrillas had been formed from many retired British soldiers who had served during the Great War and many of the Irish volunteers (terrorists) would fight locally within their own counties as they were very familiar with the local landscape and they also knew the local population. They would carry out ambushes on government forces and would disappear as quickly as they had appeared they would easily melt back into the local population. They were most effective at ambushing members of the British Army and the police. The terrorist groups had the hearts and minds of the local population the Police struggled to win the hearts and minds of the population. In May 1921 Fred was on his trusted mount "George" his horse was named after King George V his trusted steed was a handsome grey he was such a placid animal and there wasn't much that would ruffle him and George would enjoy himself most when the Regiment was on deployment in the vast countryside on the other hand Fred wasn't as keen as George. During the many forays into the countryside man and horse would live and sleep together and each trooper would have to put their mounts before themselves as they would have to sign for their horse from the Regimental

Quartermaster's department and it was every trooper's responsibility to look after their mount. The Regiment had always looked resplendent in their uniforms riding their immaculate looking horses. On one of their deployments it was in the county of Westmeath the county is slap bang in the middle of Ireland it is a very agricultural region the landscape was well suited to mounted cavalry each trooper could see for miles when mounted on their horses the Regimental Officers would scour the land through their military issued binoculars and they could survey so much of the land sprawling out before them and with the issued binoculars they were able to see so much further than the ordinary trooper. Whenever the Regiment proceeded across vast swathes of land they would ride in traditional cavalry column and sometimes they would operate in extensive drives and that way they would quickly cover miles of ground and could flush out those who were hiding in the fields. Fred would sit astride George with his carbine in its holster the rifle would also be strapped securely onto his saddle. Fred always felt extremely exposed during these particular operations covering any open ground because a highly skilled IRA sniper could see a mounted trooper from a distance and could take out a soldier and then could so easily disappear and then merge within the countryside and on some occasions they would attack the military and hide a rifle, ammunition and other bomb making material in hides after disposing of the various items of weaponry the terrorists would disappear and would be so easily blend into a local village or farmstead. Whenever a mounted column moved away from the open countryside they would have to travel along mettle roads and sometimes the inhabitants of a small farm or settlement would stop and stare at the mounted Calvary on their horses some of the inhabitants would often feed and water the horses. The Irish are well known to be horse people and they know so much about horses but sometimes they weren't as friendly towards the soldiers it was the horses they cared the most about. The Regimental Officers were well aware some not all of the inhabitants would be making a mental note of the strength of the troopers and their many different types of weapons the soldiers would be carrying and more importantly they would make a note of what direction the unit would take when they left the settlement, the information would be quickly relayed to the local IRA Commander and ironically they would then cross the countryside at speed riding horses without any of the wonderful trappings the Army Horses had they were as affective when crossing the countryside. Whenever the Regiment had been briefed by British Intelligence regarding an area the unit were about to search for any known dissidents. The Regiment would always send a few mounted soldiers to scout ahead of the main column while the remaining troopers would surround an area as best they could ensuring that any suspects who would try to make their escape across open land would soon be spotted by the main column and would subsequently be caught. At the same time if there were country roads in the area the roads would have one of the machine gun teams covering any potential escape routes or they would stop any terrorist reinforcements from arriving. It is said that an armed soldier on horseback would look extremely intimidating and a horse can cover vast tracks of land and very quickly. When the Regiment was deployed on operations searches were carried out almost on a daily basis and they were often deployed on searches to apprehend known "wanted" men on a particular operation several important terrorists had been apprehended the troopers had been deployed on this particular operation for eleven days they had been deployed deep in the countryside solely to apprehend "wanted" men and during the time Fred had smelt really badly of horse as the troopers had only been able to wash and shave on deployment and none of the men had the luxury of having a bath if they were fortunate enough and had come across a river or a stream they might be able to have a soak. During this deployment, the Regiment had come across a fast-flowing River. The officers had only allowed the troopers to bathe a troop at a time whilst the remainder had to be extremely vigilant and had to stand guard against a possible terrorist ambush and for those soldiers fortunate enough to take a dip in the river it was a bonus and an extremely rare luxury. Fred thought if George could get into the river at the same time as himself he would. As soon as those who were bathing had finished it was then that their horses were let loose into the river they seemed to enjoy having a good soaking just as their mounts had. When George was frolicking in the water he looked towards Fred and it was as though he was laughing at him, well who knows he probably was laughing as the horses had worked so hard in the sun. At the same time Fred had no idea that by spending time serving in the British Army and having served in Ireland would eventually have such a huge impact on him and his future generations. In June 1921 the Regiment, B and Headquarters Squadron were deployed to Belfast in Northern Ireland they had been sent there as escort duty for King George V, the regiments Colonel in Chief. The King was visiting Belfast to open the very first Parliament of Northern Ireland. The troop train transporting elements of the regiment to Dublin had been deliberately derailed. Two of the Regiments troopers and many of the horses had been killed and some the horses had to be put down by their handlers because of their injuries and the troopers were extremely upset at having to put their mounts out of their misery. After the derailment, the Regiment picked themselves up and were once again sent out on operations. Luckily the Royal Hussars were well accustomed to the lay of the land in Ireland as they had previously served in the Irish countryside prior to the uprising in Dublin they had served in Ireland in 1896. Much later in 1921 during his tour of duty in Ireland and unprecedently Fred had been given a spot of leave to travel to Hull and the reason was it enabled him the time to marry his beloved May and it wasn't something that had been taken lightly by the Commanding Officer more so as he had recently gone AWOL prior to the Regiment's deployment to Ireland and indeed it had been such a rare decision there were many serving soldiers who thought it had been a bad decision. On the 21st of December 1921 May and Fred were eventually married it had been a small wedding and it was also tinged with some sadness as Peter, Fred's father wasn't there to see his eldest son get married Fred had always remembered about his father and he had never forgotten him. The pair did not have the time for a traditional honeymoon and so had remained at home it was a small house in Walcott street, Hessle road. May's father was a painter and decorator so he and Fred had spent a couple of days painting the house from top to bottom to help freshen it up and at the time the cost of paint was very expensive most houses were wallpapered rather than painted because it was slightly cheaper. Fred had managed to scrape together some extra money it was just enough to purchase a second-hand bed and some other furnishings it was a valiant attempt to turn the house into a home. Fred had a week's leave and soon his leave was at an end he would have to start the long journey back to Dublin. He had to catch a troopship which was leaving Liverpool in the New Year. Fred and May had married far too quickly and the marriage had been such a rushed affair and there hadn't been any thought given to their future and to the fact that Fred was still serving in the Army currently deployed over in Ireland and he hadn't a clue about how long he would be expected to serve in Ireland. It was only the start of many problems for the newlyweds and there were so many things that could go wrong for the pair of them. Immediately from the start of the marriage everything seemed to be stacked against the newlyweds at the time the Army did not provide service men's married accommodation and as a married man Fred was required to sleep in the single accommodation block at Curragh Camp. The Regiment had initially been accommodated in Hare Park camp and soon had to move to another camp as the current camp was to become an internment camp to house the many terrorist prisoners. For every soldier serving away from home the mail was the single most important morale booster for them it was an awful feeling when a soldier doesn't receive post from home. Fred would frequently write home whenever he would have a break from his military duties. But, sadly for Fred, he never did receive any mail in reply to his many letters he had written. Very soon the situation began to get Fred down and he began to have some very dark moments and dark thoughts and it wasn't a very good situation to find oneself in especially since he was serving away from home on operations. His fellow troopers were dependent on Fred to cover them once they were exposed to any terrorist incident. Whenever he saw the post orderly enter the accommodation block and began to distribute the mail to the other soldiers Fred would always get his hopes up that he would receive a letter from home he would be very sad when once again hadn't received any mail from home. He would never let anyone see just how disappointed he was especially when he would watch the others sit on their beds to read the comforting messages from home. He soon realised there was something seriously wrong at home he had initially thought May might have been ill he then thought no that can't be the case as he knew his mum would have been in contact with him if she had been taken ill or if something more serious had happened to her. The issue regarding the lack of mail was reported to his troop sergeant he had been made aware of the sudden change in Fred's persona some of the other soldiers had let the sergeant know. Fred was one of the more reliable soldiers and he was very well liked within the troop. Fred had begun to walk about the billet and outside the building but within the camp area he had looked as though he had suddenly got the world's problems resting on top of his shoulders. The postal orderly had informed the troop sergeant Sergeant Smith regarding the lack of mail for Fred and some of the other soldiers within the billet had mentioned the change in Fred's personality and persona to the troop sergeant. The Troop Sergeant had diligently informed the Squadron Sergeant Major (SSM) of the changes in Fred's persona. The SSM informed the troop sergeant he would have to talk to Fred but it would be better in his office and before informing the Officer Commanding (OC) of the ongoing situation in-regards to Fred. It was very important to find what was going on in Fred's head because if he was deployed on any future operations he could become a serious liability to the other troops especially on counter insurgency patrols and more importantly the SSM had to get to the bottom of the situation before Fred became an even more dangerous liability to others who would have to rely on him to carry out his job in very hazardous conditions the SSM had to rectify the situation and soon. A soldier can become a very dangerous liability to himself and his comrades in any combat situation but on the flip side he might also be trying to work his ticket and he might be trying to get a hospital move back home? Before the SSM could see him, Fred had received a letter from Hull and he hadn't recognised the handwriting on the envelope and so had prepared himself for some bad news and he sat on his bed to read the letter. He had tentatively opened the envelope and he was dreading reading the contents he soon established it was a letter written by a friend of his wife her friend hadn't signed the letter and hadn't written down her address. The letter went on to explain what Fred had thought all along and the news was exactly what he had been dreading the friend had gone on to explain that May had been having an affair and it had taken place immediately after he had left for Ireland. Fred wasn't at all shocked it was just the bluntness of the letter and had hit him the hardest the information had hurt him greatly and he soon began to feel like he was such a bloody fool. While he was still based in Ireland he was powerless to do anything about the situation he now found himself in it wasn't as though he could just drop everything and go home to try and sort out this problem it was never going to happen he was serving in the Army and it wasn't a charity or a benevolent organisation he had to just get on with things as best he could. In 1921 a divorce was extremely expensive and it would be very difficult to have his marriage annulled as he would have to wait for the required minimum of two years to file for a divorce and at the same time he would have to plead poverty to the courts and at the time it had only been the rich in society who could afford the costs of a divorce. He had felt so helpless and here he was in Ireland and on operations without the means to get himself back across the Irish Sea. The more he had read the letter the more he became extremely angry with himself for rushing into the marriage and for being a such a bloody fool at the same time he was feeling extremely sorry for himself. The sergeant had seen Fred sat on his bed and told him that he was to see the Sergeant Major immediately Fred fastened the top button of his jacket and placed his cap onto his head and proceeded to march out of the accommodation block together with the troop sergeant who was by now marching behind him Fred and he began barking out the words of command and he had ordered

Fred to march very smartly they were about to cross the Regimental parade square and it was a bit of a no no under no circumstances is anyone in the Army to walk or amble across the Regimental parade square. They had to smartly march across the vast open space of the parade square!! there is no place to hide and once a soldier takes a foot onto the parade square it is open to many prying eyes Fred's troop offices were situated in the far corner of the parade square. As the sergeant marched Fred towards the troop office there were other members of the troop who were observing the way Fred was being treated as the pair reached halfway across the parade square the RSM (Regimental Sergeant Major) had seen the pair marching on his parade square and as soon as he saw them he quickly grabbed hold of his best riding crop and rushed out of his office and onto the edge of the square and as he did so he marched extremely smartly and began to bellow "oi you horrible looking pair what the bloody hell do you think you are doing setting foot on my parade square? get over here right now and at the double". The sergeant shouted out the words of command "quick march" and the pair smartly marched towards the RSM. They had marched as though their lives had depended upon it and the RSM had watched each drill movement as though it was a drill competition. Once the pair were stood in front of him the sergeant bellowed the words of command "halt" and both Fred and the sergeant simultaneously slammed their boots hard into the ground and came to a perfect military halt. The RSM spoke "that's much better I do like to see smart soldiers in the Regiment performing precise sharp drill movements I hate sloppiness do I make myself clear". He looked at sergeant Smith and shouted, "why are you marching Trooper Peterson on my bloody parade square?" The sergeant began to explain about the squadron sergeant major wanting to see trooper Peterson outside his office for personal reasons. The

RSM approached Fred and began to look him up and down as if he was inspecting him and to make sure he looked spick and span and was dressed correctly the RSM suddenly responded "ok carry on I don't want to see any bloody sloppy drill movements I shall be watching the pair of you do you hear me?" Sergeant Smith had acknowledged what the RSM had said and with that the pair began to march away from the RSM with Sergeant Smith once more barking out the drill commands. They soon arrived at the squadron offices the SSM's office was situated in one of the four offices along a corridor at the heart of the building. At the far end was the Officer Commanding's (OC) opulent office and next to the sergeant major's office was the Squadron clerk's office including the second in commands (2IC) room. Sergeant Smith knocked loudly on the SSM's door as he couldn't just walk in as protocol deemed that he would have to knock and wait to be invited in. Once he knocked on the door a booming voice emanating from within the office "enter" the sergeant quickly opened the door and marched himself in and ensuring he had shut the door behind him. He spoke to the SSM and starting to explain all about Trooper Peterson and his "personal" problems. The sergeant major was an old and bold soldier he had enlisted into the Army as a "boy" soldier at the age of sixteen and together with his experiences he knew every trick there was in the book and in the past, he had used some of the same excuses himself. The sergeant went back into the corridor and began to bark out the words of command and Fred came to attention and marched himself into the SSM's office just as he began to march into the SSM's office the Officer Commanding (OC) stepped out of his office and enquired about what the commotion was all about sergeant Smith was about to explain when the SSM decided to step out of his office and into the corridor and asked the, OC if he could explain about the situation before him in his own office and in private he would explain what was going on. At the same time Fred was told to stand down and to wait back in the corridor after ten minutes the SSM had left the OC's office. As he approached Fred Sergeant Smith shouted out the words of command and brought Fred to attention and the SSM told Fred to stand at ease. The SSM entered his office and shouted "sergeant Smith march Trooper Peterson back in" As Fred smartly marched back into the office he could see that the SSM was sat at his desk and he came to a halt in front of the SSM's desk Fred and he could see that the office was very sparse in a military sense of the word the SSM had various items of militaria he had collected over his military service and it had ranged from his service in South Africa, The North West Frontier he also had various items from his Great War service and there were several photographs of himself in full uniform. There were many military photographs as photography had become very popular around 1855 during the Crimea war and many military men had enjoyed having their pictures taken in their uniform. Fred was still standing to attention and in front of the SSM he was waiting for the SSM to tell him why he had been summoned mind you Fred had a very good idea why. The SSM was sat wearing his best Regimental jacket the jacket was adorned with various medal ribbons including The Queens South Africa Medal, The Kings South Africa Medal and his three Great War medal ribbons and they consisted of the 1914 star (Mons Star), The Allied Victory medal, more commonly known as "pip, squeak and Wilfrid". The SSM had served in the Army for almost twenty years and by now he should have retired after The Great War had ended but once the war had ended there were thousands of ex service personnel who had been demobbed following armistice the Regiment had found itself severely understrength and soon after the Regiment had returned to England there had to be a huge recruitment drive to bring the Regiment back up to war strength so many soldiers from the 5th Hussars had helped to bolster the ranks of the Royal Hussars and had helped to bring the Regiment back up to operational strength. The SSM had been requested to remain with the Regiment to help train the new recruits and as soon as the Regiment was up to strength the commanding officer had received orders from the War Office to deploy to Ireland by April 1920. The SSM was once again offered the chance to remain with the Regiment to take him up to his retirement after the Regiments deployment to Ireland and he had obviously grabbed at the opportunity with both hands as he had known nothing else since joining the Army at sixteen. Fred had a very good idea why he had been summoned by the Sergeant Major and it wasn't for a nice chat and a pleasant cup of tea. The Army wasn't a namby pamby organisation he knew the Sergeant Major would be seriously concerned about his abilities and his current state of mind as he would have to ensure that he wasn't a liability to other members of the Regiment. The Sergeant Major then spoke "what the fuck is going on Peterson, I hear you are pining for your loved one back home is that correct?" Fred responded, "yes sir", the SSM replied "well whatever it is get it out of your fucking system even if it means you getting pissed and going on a bender I just can't have a soldier going out on patrol and isn't fully focused on the task at hand do I make myself bloody clear Peterson be it on your fucking head because if you get one of my men killed I won't say what will happen to you? I hope I make myself perfectly clear?" Fred once again replied, "yes Sir perfectly clear". Suddenly the SSM bellowed at sergeant Smith "now get this fucking excuse of a soldier out of my sight I don't wish to hear any more of his bull shit now take him out and beast him on the parade square it will give him some more time to think and to clear his head of his bloody shit" The sergeant replied, "yes sir" and marched Fred out of the Squadron building. Sergeant Smith was dreading having to march Fred again and across the parade square for a beasting, a beasting is soldier slang for having to spend hours on the parade square carrying out many marching movements, as he knew the RSM would be looking from his window. Other members of the Regiment could see that Fred was once again being marched across the parade square and they could see he was once again receiving a beasting. There was nowhere for either of them to hide from the many prying eyes. The sergeant barked out words of command and at the same time he spoke to Fred in a lower tone his voice was almost at a whisper and all of sudden sergeant Smith reduced his voice to a hiss he told Fred what he thought of him including his silly domestic issues back home. Fred had all the time in the world to think about his domestic situation and he told himself he would divorce May just as soon as he had saved enough money for a quick divorce and if he couldn't find the money he would have to wait for two years without having any contact with May or so he thought. After his time on the parade square Fred returned to the billet he was drenched in his sweat and although he was fit and kept himself in shape but having a beasting on the parade square for an hour would take it out on any soldiers even if they were extremely fit the sergeant had to be seen to carry out the many drill movements correctly as he knew he had been watched by the various Regimental Officers including the main man in the Regiment the RSM. Fred quickly took a bath and changed into his fatigue dress because later that afternoon the squadron were to deploy to the local rifle ranges to carry out weapon drills and live firing on Curragh ranges. The machine gun team were going to provide a live fire demonstration with the Hotchkiss heavy machine guns to the Squadron. The Commanding Officer had deemed every trooper within the

Regiment would need to know the basic operations of the machine gun in case a member of the machine gun team was either wounded or killed on operations. The machine gun was an extremely important tool to put down suppressing fire on an enemy whilst the rest of the Regiment attacked from the front and the flanks. So, it was why the Regiments Commanding Officer had ordered that any trooper would replace the machine gun crew and could provide suppressing fire on the enemy with the machine guns. Fred hadn't liked firing the heavy guns in fact most troopers didn't like operating the machine guns. The squadron had soon arrived at the ranges the range was close by and as they approached the ranges they could see two of the Heavy machine guns' they were already setup and were slightly away from the main range area the machine gun team took a few of the troopers at a time and instructed them on how to strip the machine guns down and to clean the various parts of the guns and reassemble them during this process they were normally timed to see how long it took for the troopers to strip and reassemble the various parts of the machine guns. The guns were very heavy beasts and even more so when the tripods were attached. It was a reliable machine gun and it was gas actuated which meant the working parts were forced to rear by the gasses from the last bullet having been fired from the barrel and the gasses would force the working parts to the rear which then fed the next round into the chamber and ready for firing the barrel was air cooled rather than having a tin of water attached by tube to cool down the barrel while it fired thousands of rounds the air stopped the barrel from overheating. To operate the gun effectively it had required a three man team one to pull the trigger and to provide effectively fire, another person to feed the ammunition belt and one to act as spotter to let the man know who was firing if the bullets were falling short. Fred had been nominated to fire the machine gun first and he began to mutter "fucking typical they know I don't like firing the bloody thing". Dotted around the butts, the butts are where the targets are raised and dropped, were some sheep roaming around behind the targets, even today many military ranges have the local sheep farmer bringing the sheep onto the ranges to chew on the grass and to keep the grass around the butts, short. Fred had been moaning and chatting to some of the other soldiers and he hadn't listened to what the range safety officer had been saying during a briefing. The range officer had ordered if any sheep were seen in and around the target area they were to immediately cease firing a warning flag would be displayed from the area of the butts, no one was to fire while the sheep were milling around the target area. Fred had already got himself into a comfortable position behind the machine gun and he was about to fire he was instructed to open fire as soon as the targets appeared in front of him, Fred saw the targets and fired the machine gun but he had mistakenly switched the safety catch to continuous fire instead of single bursts of fire and all of a sudden the barrel of the machine gun pulled up and in to the air as it did so he lost control of the machine gun and the bullets spewed from the barrel of the machine gun skywards and as it did so a large sheep had appeared around some mounds just above the butts and directly behind Fred's target and he pulled the trigger he could see as though it was in slow motion the bullets had hit the sheep and all of a sudden a large red patch appeared on one side of the sheep's fleece turned a dark red and the animal toppled over behind a small mound. Suddenly someone began to kick Fred in the leg he was about to curse at whoever had kicked him and just as he looked up from the machine gun he could see it was the range officer "bloody hell son didn't you fucking hear what I just said?" Fred replied "no sir I was concentrating so hard on the target" the time there was a group of men who had worked alongside the military range staff and they were the civilian range staff they were stood around the range area and they were laughing at Fred's unfortunate accident a few minutes later a local farm hand arrived at the ranges he had accessed the open range area and he was riding on a very manky looking horse he t began shouting at the soldiers "what the fuck do you thick Brits think you fucking are doing? you have killed more of our bloody sheep than you have killed IRA men " Fred thought "bloody hell I don't need this crap it's just what I don't need the bloody range officer on my back my life is going to be even more shitty". Luckily for Fred the range officer didn't want to take matters any further as he had put it down to an accident the farmer would eventually be compensated. Fred could hear his SSM in the distance cursing and swearing at him all he could hear was "Peterson you won't hear the last of this fucking shit do you bloody hear me" and that was it he knew the sort of tasty words the SSM would be using and in his head Fred thought "oh why don't you put a bloody sock in it you fucking dick head". The soldiers had to collect the brass casings from the spent bullets and hand the brass to the civilian range staff. It would be many years later when the British Forces had submitted a report post deployment to Ireland during 1920-1921 the report was submitted to the War Office and it had covered the Irish War of Independence it had been found that many range staff working for the British Army at the time would scour the Army ranges and recover vast amounts of live ammunition and would supply the IRA with the ammunition that was found around the various range areas. Fred was a very good soldier but his private life was beginning to affect his military life. The military way of life and civilian domestic life at the time were an extremely toxic mix. He had learnt an extremely important lesson it had made him think more seriously about himself and

May and he had decided not to let his private life interfere with his military life he knew his marriage was over and there was absolutely nothing he could do about his current situation he found himself in yes it was very frustrating. He figured out there was nothing left to save in the marriage since he had realised May might have been having an affair up to the day of their marriage and deep within his heart something had now died inside him. From that moment on he knew exactly what he needed to do and it was certainly wasn't to become the centre of attention in the Regiment if he continued to be the centre of attention during his service life in Ireland it would become even more worse than it already was. Fred continued to read the letter that had been sent by May's friend and read it repeatedly until he began to think May might have been having an affair soon after their wedding as the lady who had sent him the letter had pointed out May had been having an affair since January 1922 it was less than a month after their marriage. This was why it had led Fred to believe that she may have been seeing the other person prior to their wedding. As mentioned Fred was unable to afford the costs of an official divorce and at the time most men would just walk away from a marriage without divorcing their wives and just re-marry. In Ireland Fred was living in very dangerous times there were dangers everywhere be it assignations, vendettas and the many murders of policemen and soldiers. The days would be full of the drama of life and death situations and many soldiers found themselves in. There were days when the troops would be stuck in barracks for long periods of time and it was so boring because the soldiers had the same daily routine starting in the mornings with room inspections and the rest of the day with drill, weapon handling, grooming of the horses and yet even more range practice. Fred finally got his head sorted out and he had decided he could not afford to pay for a quick divorce which meant May would not be able to marry even if she wanted to. This fact had made Fred feel a little better about his own situation and he thought "if I am in Ireland doing this kind of shit every day then May would suffer too". It would serve two purposes one May could stew in her own pig shit and two it would keep the Squadron Sergeant Major and the Troop Sergeant off his back. The routine would also help him take the thoughts of her adultery from his mind and help him to deal with everyday things until he was ready to deal with the divorce situation as soon as he arrived back in England. He knew his time would come and it would be on his own terms.

Chapter 4 - Leave

During another one of Fred's extremely rare breaks from soldering in Ireland, in almost two years he had managed to obtain permission to go home on leave twice. On his current batch of leave he had much he had needed to sort out in Hull. But on this current break from the regiment he was going to let his hair down and relax the business in Hull could wait just a little bit longer as he felt that he needed some time to wind down before facing his many and growing domestic issues. He had arranged to stay in Liverpool for a while and he was going to make sure that he was going to enjoy himself. As he waited to board the troop ship taking him back home across the vastness of the Irish sea. At the dockside in Dublin he stood in silence as he watched many troops who had been injured being loaded onto the troop ship and other soldiers had also stood in silence and they too were watching the many injured soldiers as they were carried on stretchers and loaded onto the ship many of the injured soldiers had been treated at the British Army hospital in Dublin and were having to be moved home for further treatment. Fred had thought to himself there go I by the grace of god the poor buggers. Once the injured had been safely loaded onto the ship he could hear in the distance a military clerk shouting out the names of the soldiers who were to board the ship the clerk was reading the names from a nominal roll it contained a list of those who were about to leave Ireland the clerk was at the same time checking each soldiers Identity Card (ID card) including their leave passes it was a document issued by the soldier's parent Regiment authorising the soldier to travel on leave. The clerks were ensuring the soldiers had been authorised to travel on leave by their respective Regiments. Fred was thinking to himself come on mate you are just being a bloody stupid bugger make it snappy there's a good chap get a move on get this ship moving most of the other soldiers waiting had the same thoughts. Once the ship had berthed in Liverpool Fred hadn't too far to travel as he was going to stay with family friends within the Liverpool docks area and then sometime later he would visit his mother and brother Edwin in Hull. As he had some very serious business to sort out in Hull one of the things on his mind was he had to find out as much information as he could about his estranged wife and as much information about her lover. His anger towards May had by now began to subside and had been replaced by a steely determination to obtain his divorce it had been driving him on. His efforts were solely concentrated on obtaining a divorce and as soon as possible. The crossing from Dublin to Liverpool had only taken six hours. On board the ship was so cramped as the old and battered troop ship hadn't been built for luxury travel. The ship had left Dublin early in the morning and had arrived at the port in Liverpool as the sun was just beginning to rise and against the bright blue sky the sun had made the port look so much better than it was. The dock area was already bustling with the many dock workers who had been offloading stores and the different bits of machinery from the many ships moored up at the dockside the scene had reminded Fred of the mornings his father would happily set off for work to the same docks and the scene had brought back the sad memories of what happened on the horrible day that his father was found floating in the Herculaneum dock he had never got over the way his father had died. As the ship berthed Fred could smell the familiar and very distinctive odors emanating from around the dockside it had added to the port puree of smells. It had seemed to him it had been a long time since the troop ship had entered the river Mersey and having then been secured at its berth. A sergeant major came onboard the ship and ordered everyone who were about to disembark to have their ID cards and leave any documents at the ready for yet another inspection there was a low murmur emanating from within the ranks it was at this point the sergeant major yelled out "now just fucking shut up and listen if you don't listen the bloody lot of you will remain onboard this ship and you will immediately travel back to Ireland with you orrible lot still on it? now do I make myself fucking clear, well do I" the troops murmured and there was a reluctant acknowledgement from the troops "yes sir" they had replied in unison Fred thought "oh no this is all we need, a fucking dick head of a sergeant major who wants to make a name for himself". The troops obediently lined up in a single file to have their documents inspected and as they knew it was far better to do as they were told because if not they could so easily end up being sent back to Ireland. So, with their kit bags and documents in hand the soldiers formed an orderly queue on the dockside with their documents ready to have them checked and they needed to make sure they had their leave documents stamped by the military clerks because without the official stamp the document could be classed as a forgery. Once Fred had disembarked from the ship he didn't have too far to walk and he felt so good as he had plenty of money burning a hole in his pocket. He had managed to find the house where he was going to stay for the duration of his stay. The family were friends of his late father Peter his dad's friend was called Albert the first thing Fred did was to pay Albert for his food and lodgings during his stay at his house he knew if he hadn't paid Albert there and then he would have ended up spending the money Fred was more than happy to pay his dues as soon as possible. The money was a god send to Albert and his family because at the time work and money was in such short supply. As soon as he was shown to his room he had unpacked his clothes from his Army issue kit bag and he took out a couple of clean shirts and a pair of trousers including his only decent pair of shoes it was everything that he had owned Albert's wife Frances kindly offered to iron Fred's clothes as they had been scrunched up inside the kitbag and were extremely crumpled. After a short while she had handed them back to him his clothes looked nicely ironed and so much better than he could have ever managed. Later Fred had offered to take Albert out for a drink to a nearby pub and when they arrived at the pub Albert introduced Fred to some of the pub's regulars and he had explained Fred was a friend of the family and he went on to point out he was Peter Peterson's son some of the men had still remembered Peter and mumbled "it was a bloody shame about what happened to your dad lad" It was at this point Albert went on to mention he was currently serving in the Army and serving over in Ireland all of a sudden the atmosphere within the pub had suddenly changed the mood had ominously changed and it was very unsettling some of the men shouted "good on ya lad" as a show of support it seemed to have lifted the sour atmosphere but there was another group of men who were drinking in a corner of the pub and they had made it very obvious that Fred wasn't welcome in the pub. One of the group shouted, "hey fucker you have over stayed your bloody welcome in here now piss off that is if you know what's good for you best you fuck off right now and don't come back here your like aren't welcome" the men were of Irish decent and would never forgive anyone who was serving in the British Army especially serving in Ireland Albert turned to Fred and told him to sup up quickly the pair quickly finished their pints and had left for another pub. Liverpool at the time had a pub on almost every street corner and punters didn't have too far to walk to find a watering hole as there were so many pubs in the area it was due to the many thirsty dock workers it was a catch

22 situation. For many of the workers the dock owners owned most of the local housing the houses had been built solely for the dock workforce and the housing had been paid for and built on behalf of the dock owners they had also owned many of the local public houses. It was quite cynical of the dock owners as they would pay the dock workers for their blood and sweat and tears in the docks and on the other hand they would fleece them for rent living in the local housing stock that surrounded the docks. The dock owners would take the workers hard earned cash in the pubs the same pubs the dock owners owned. In many ways, they would soon have their money back lining their pockets and so the cycle would continue and the cycle of poverty but it was also business and business men aren't a charity. The pair soon found themselves another Pub they had a few drinks and left the pub a few hours later very much the worse for wear and on their way out they had purchased a couple of bottles of stout and had carefully placed them into their jacket pockets and as they had meandered down the road it was the same road that would eventually lead to Alberts home as they were walking home both had a cigarette dangling from their mouths. they were very tipsy but merry and happy before arriving home some of the local kids began to run around the pair shouting, "av ya got any sweets mister" Albert shouted, "bugger off bloody beggars get back home it's far too bloody late to be playing outside and harassing me now go before I give you a bloody clip around the ear" as the pair carried on walking home one of the kids shouted, "ah piss off mister". When the pair eventually entered Alberts house they were hit by the wonderful smells of something nice cooking in the kitchen whatever it was it had smelt delicious. It hadn't helped having a belly full of ale the hallway was full of the gorgeous smells coming from the direction of the kitchen. Albert and Fred said in unison "ah something smells nice Frances?" As

they walked into the kitchen she was stood in the kitchen stirring a pot of meat and she had seemed slightly annoyed she said, "where the bloody hell have you two been? as if I needed to ask, now the pair of you sit down I have a lovely rabbit stew bubbling away on the stove" Albert suddenly grabbed hold of Frances around her waist, she brushed him off and shouted at him "not now we have a guest". She placed the stew into bowls and set two wooden spoons on the table as the couple couldn't afford posh metal cutlery so Albert would whittle some pieces of wood to make wooden cutlery. The stew looked great and it had smelt fantastic to compliment the meal they drank two more bottles of stout Albert told Frances to get three jam jars and as soon as she had placed the jam jars on the kitchen table he poured a drop of stout for her and all three of them sat around the kitchen table Fred spoke first "ah to good friends and a meal fit for a king what more does a man need". She giggled and said, "oh Fred you are so silly" they giggled and all three laughed out loud, more so the men it may have been something to do with the amount of ale they had consumed. Fred felt so good especially after the many months of soldiering in Ireland and having to constantly be on alert especially out on patrol he was always in a state of heightened anxiety once back in barracks the monotony and the many contradictions of life in barracks the tedious routine. Life felt so different now away for the Army environment it had felt so good to be able to just relax. At that precise moment, his life felt so good the evening shared with Albert and Frances had made it feel that much better they didn't have much but what they did have they had shared it with him. The money Fred had given them would help to make their lives just that little bit easier. The following morning Fred went to visit his father's grave over at St James's cemetery, it is close to the Anglican cathedral, to where his father Peter had been buried in 1917. Fred had also managed to visit some of his old friends he had known all of them previously they hadn't seen one another for almost two years. Within the city centre there was some animosity shown towards British troops that were serving in Ireland. One evening Fred had gone out for the evening to one of the local pubs in the Toxteth area together with some of his old friends and it was while he was in one of the pubs he was introduced to a local girl she came from the Dingle area. She was a brunette and was very petite her eyes were of a deep emerald colour. It was her eyes that had caught Fred's gaze he had been transfixed by her looks. She may have been tiny but she had certainly made up for her size by her razor sharp tongue. Her name was Sarah and she had a very quick sense of humour which Fred had liked that in her. Sarah had suddenly laughed out very loud she had almost spat out the half pint of mild that she had been drinking, Fred responded "what's so bloody funny?" Sarah replied, "it's your name? Fred had told her his first name was Rodmond it is a Scandinavian name but he had preferred to use his family name of "Fred". Sarah spluttered what sort of name is that? Do you have a middle name?" Fred replied, "yes my middle name is Fred why?" Sarah replied, "OK from now on I shall call you Freddie" Fred was quick to respond, "oh so there is to be a next time then? that's great news" Sarah hadn't responded to his comment and had continued to drink her half of mild. Over Fred's leave period he and Sarah had become something of an "item" he had continued to see her on a regular basis. Sarah hadn't introduced him to her parents George and Annie as there was a very good reason for not introducing him more especially to her father it could wait for another time. The issue with her father would eventually test their strength for one another. Her parents were second generation Irish and they were Roman Catholics and at the time neither of them had believed in divorce nor inter faith marriage and of course there was the additional issue of Fred serving with the British Army and of all things serving in Ireland. Sarah and Fred had some extremely serious problems on the horizon now it was all in the future as the relationship hadn't yet got off the ground all those issues would have to wait because Fred had a much more serious and by far a more important issue that he would have to resolve within his own family it had everything to do with his estranged wife May and their divorce. The political and social life in the 1920's was a much more different world to what it is in the 21st century. During this period, the United Kingdom was a country of vast contradictions for instance it had a vast empire and with it came the vast riches of the world all at the feet of the British Empire the period was sometimes referred to as the "swinging twenties" and the world economy was entering a period of severe depression it was also a period of mass unemployment across the country. Some of the rich in society had lost vast fortunes on the stock market and many had been thoroughly disgraced and sadly many had resorted to committing suicide rather facing the disgrace and the embarrassment of losing everything. One could say that Fred had been one of the more fortunate ones in Britain serving in the British Army not that he would have thought that of himself for instance he was housed, fed and watered and after any deductions from his pay packet he had a little money left over in his pocket and at the time he hadn't felt he was very fortunate far from it. Fred had earnt twelve shillings a week of Army pay before any deductions and he was paid some additional pay such as extreme or specialist pay of between three pence or sixpence a day. One could not say Fred had wined and dined Sarah during his spot of leave in Liverpool but what he had done was to make her feel very special he had looked after her just like a true gentleman and so much better than she was used to. Each time they had met during his leave they would visit the local hostelries. Every time he had gone out during his leave he would have to carry his ID card including his leave pass and he would also carry his pay book for additional identification. At the same time in Liverpool and Manchester the Irish Republican Army Volunteers were very active and he was very aware that he could be stopped and asked to prove who he was by the police. There were so many soldiers who had not returned to their Regiments in Ireland after they had a bout of leave and they hadn't returned for obvious reasons. It was soon time for Fred to go and visit his mum Susan and his younger brother Edwin in Hull. While in Hull he would have to find out as much information as could regarding his wife's adultery and he would need to collect as much information as he could and anything he could find out regarding the man she was living with. May's infidelities and her various shenanigans had to be noted so he would have enough evidence to put before a divorce court. Fred had caught the cross-Pennine train from Lime street to Hull when he arrived at the station in Hull Fred had walked from the railway station to his mum's house as it wasn't far he had brought Susan a nice bunch of flowers as she loved flowers. He knocked on the front door Susan was by nature a very cheerful person and as she had opened the front door to peer out of she could see it had been Fred who was stood in front of her with his Army kit bag and a very large bunch of flowers wrapped up in brown paper and all of a sudden she burst into tears and said "oh Freddy it's you oh sweetheart please come inside I have missed you so much" Fred could hear Edwin in a back room and whenever Edwin became over excited he couldn't talk so he would try to make noises the sounds were almost grunting noises he had recognised Fred's voice. Fred gave Susan a kiss on her cheek and walked into the parlour to where Edwin was sat in his home made "pram" he was so excited he could tell it had been Fred who had entered the room Fred bent down and kissed Edwin on the forehead and had wheeled him into the kitchen where by now Susan had made a lovely refreshing pot of tea and she had poured three mugs of tea she had poured some tea for Edwin in his mug and had added a little extra milk in to Edwin's mug to make sure that the tea was lukewarm to ensure he didn't end up burning his throat and the mug hadn't been filled to the brim as he would often spill the majority of the contents all over his clothes due to his involuntary and his very erratic arm movements Fred had sat talking to both of them about his recent adventures over in Ireland and the subject of May had soon come up in conversation Susan had told him that May had moved out of the family home. There was also the matter of some back rent and it needed to be paid to the landlord Fred was aware and had managed to save some of his pay to go towards the outstanding rent he was also able to send a little rent money to Susan it was on top of an allowance he had been sending for Susan and Edwin to ease his mother's burden. He said to his mum that first thing in the morning he would be going around to the house and would move everything out of the house and he would pay the landlord the remainder of the rent that he owed. Susan had informed Fred of the where about of May and how he could find her now she was living with another man Fred had made a note of the address. His mother said, "son please don't go around to the house promise me please she isn't worth it everyone in the area knows about the affair and what she has done to you and she has been ostracized by her neighbours and you a man who is serving his country". Fred replied, "its ok mam the pair of them will get what is coming to them and it won't be me doing it", he wrote the man's name in his little notebook that he was collecting information on as he could he would need to collect enough hard and factual evidence for any future court proceedings the problem was he would need to collect as much factual evidence concerning her adultery. It would all go towards helping his case when it came to be heard in the divorce court. He still couldn't afford to pay for a divorce. Divorces at the time were deemed only for the rich as it was only the rich who could afford the cost of a divorce. Fred enquired to where Henry was Susan had told him that he had travelled to Liverpool to attend a funeral for once of his relatives Susan hadn't attended as it would be too much to take Edwin as well so Henry had gone on his own. Fred had to reluctantly bide his time and it was soon time for him to return to Liverpool and board the troop ship to return to Ireland. He had managed to get himself a lift across the Pennines and onwards to Liverpool Susan had cried her eyes out when Fred had left he had made sure that his mum had some extra pennies for her and Edwin. Edwin seemed to sense his mum was upset and he had held her hand and Fred had given Edwin a kiss on his forehead and just as he was saying his goodbyes a lorry had driven into the road and it had stopped outside of the house it was Fred's lift the truck had various crates in the rear of the truck as the driver had to deliver them to one of the many docks in Liverpool. The truck was soon heading out of Hull and onto the main road heading west towards Manchester and then onto Liverpool. As soon as he had arrived in Liverpool he quickly headed to the dock where the troopship was berthed as he had to check on the sailing date as sometimes the ships would leave a day early or perhaps a couple of days later it had all depended on the Captain of the ship and the tides. He walked to the docks and could see the troop ship in the distance it was already berthed once at the dock he had entered a wooden cabin which was at the side of the dock he spoke to a military clerk who was sitting at a desk Fred needed to know when the next troopship was sailing for Dublin the clerk had confirmed the ship would be sailing in 2 days' time the clerk had made a note of Fred's details on a nominal role he had also made another note confirming that Fred had been informed of the date and the time of when the ship was due to sail for Ireland. Fred still didn't know where his "latest" girlfriend was living as she hadn't felt brave enough to let him know there was also a very strong possibility he would never get to know her address but it had been extremely fortunate that he had bumped into one of Sarah's friends and had spoken to her about his need to meet the lady he fancied and couldn't get out of his head. He asked her friend to let her know he would like to meet her later the same evening in the pub they had first met. That evening Sarah duly turned up at the same pub he hadn't had any idea if her friend had managed to pass on his message to her, obviously she had he had a dirty great big smile on his face she was smiling but it was also tinged with a sense of sadness as she knew he would have to go back to Ireland very soon. They decided to go into the snug area of the pub it was so much private than the main bar area. It was tonight that he was going to tell her everything about his marriage to May and he then took a deep breath and began to tell Sarah everything about his marriage all of a sudden the blood seemed to have drained from her face it had turned pure white and she could only whisper "oh fuck that's all I need how am I going to explain this to me ma and pa" He asked her "is there anything wrong?" she blurted "wrong for fucks sake it couldn't be any worse" he replied, "what do you mean" Sarah screamed at him "you're a bloody protestant for one, married and a British soldier and serving in bloody Ireland you really don't understand do you Fred it is bad it really is so bad for me and for us? I just don't know how this relationship is ever going to survive" he sat in the snug not knowing what to say he began to think that their Virginian relationship was dead in the water. Sarah calmly said,

Leave

"Freddy you must know by my Irish surname surely even you can't be that stupid? or can you?" he said, "you don't sound Irish to me" oh how he laughed loudly at own his silly joke but in his mind, he thought that he was so funny it had more to do with his nerves. She had mentioned her parents were still travelling to Ireland to visit various relatives over there. At that moment in time he didn't care what her parents did or what they thought of the pair of them seeing one another. At that precise moment, he had only just realised he was falling head over heels for this tiny feisty lady who was sat in front of him and it was becoming one of those whirlwind romances. He was sailing the very next morning for Ireland and this was going to be his last evening of freedom for a very long time. He asked her if she would kindly write to him while he was still stationed over in Ireland she had agreed that she would. He wrote his military address on a page from his notebook and ripped the page from the notebook with his address written on it and then handed the piece of paper to her she seemed to be a little teary and to the outside world the relationship hadn't a hope in hell's chance of working certainly if her parents had found out about their illicit liaison they would have immediately nipped the relationship in the bud. Sarah would have to hide Fred's address or give it to one of her trusted friends. He offered to walk her home she had initially said no but after thinking about his offer to walk her home she said "yes you can Freddy but only part of the way" he said well I suppose it is better than nothing and as they walked along the cobbled streets she suddenly stopped him under a street light and told him that it was far enough and she, explained to him "I cannot afford to have anyone from around here seeing us together please try to understand my situation?" they kissed and as he turned to walk back to Albert's house she shouted "please look after yourself over there Freddy" he replied "I will sweetheart I will, I promise" she remained under the street light until he had disappeared from view. The following morning after he had eaten a hearty breakfast Fred began the walk to the docks area to where the troop ship was berthed. The military order was for each soldier to travel in Military uniform and Fred had felt as proud as punch as he walked through the streets proudly wearing his uniform. As he walked along the dock road various people had spat at him some had spat on the footpath as they looked at him full of hatred in their eyes there were many families of Irish decent and that had included Sarah's family especially her father George he had been against everything the British Army were doing in Ireland. Fred had soon arrived at the shipping office and once again he had to register he could board the ship and at the quayside there was a holding area where each soldier travelling to Ireland had to muster before embarking on board the troop ship. The ship was currently being loaded with stores intended for the military based in Ireland. As Fred began to book in a clerk asked him if he had a good leave? and his reply was "interesting, very interesting indeed". The ship was finally ready to sail and there were several soldiers who had been unaccounted for and the Royal Military Police had called out the roll three more times and still the soldiers were missing and couldn't be accounted for and eventually the troops had been given permission to board the ship. By the time the ship had slipped out of the river Mersey and began to head out into the Irish it was by now pitch black and most of the troops had managed to get a little sleep. Sleep was another of the basic needs of a soldier the other was food. The ship had finally arrived in Ireland where it had berthed at the far end of the Dublin docks. There were a few of the Regimental vehicles waiting to take the troops onwards to Curragh camp where once again Fred would join his Regiment and his troop. Those who were serving with the Royal Hussars were greeted at the guardroom by the Regimental Police Sergeant who had lined up the troopers and had taken great pleasure from marching the troopers straight onto the Regimental parade square and proceeded to put them through their paces with some marching drill Fred was already pissed off he had only been back at the Regiment for less than an hour and he had thought this is bloody typical nothing ever changes around here. After the spot of drill the soldiers were dismissed to join their respective troops. Fred was still fuming and he thought "I know where I would rather be and it isn't here in bloody Ireland". Believe it or not there was a plus side to all the bull shit Sarah stuck to her promise and started to regularly write to Fred and it hadn't gone un-noticed by his fellow comrades and more especially by his troop sergeant it was very noticeable to everyone Fred was getting back to his old self again he hadn't been a worry and hadn't been a headache to his superiors. In Liverpool Sarah had to be ultra-careful her father George or even her mother Annie didn't find out about what she was getting up to. Sarah had asked one of her closest friends if Fred could use her address to send his letters to and everything had been agreed regarding his correspondence. She had informed him of the friends address the one he was to use when exchanging correspondence with her. The problem for any soldier serving at the time and it includes soldier's serving in today's modern Army there are many intense periods of operations and of sustained combat but there are so many more periods of pure boredom and having to carry out the same old daily routines of drill, weapon training and exercises. The soldier often feels being in barracks can be extremely tedious and unnecessary and benign but for the officers it is a form of self-discipline and it is bad form to have soldiers becoming lazy and lethargic within any military environment. It is during the many periods of boredom during the mundane and monotonous routine when the ordinary soldier gets himself into so much trouble be it frequenting the local hostelries or fighting each other back in barracks. The Royal Military Police are kept very busy during these periods when troops are based for long periods in camp. During the British Army's time in Ireland it had been the jurisdiction of the Royal Military Police to apprehend and arrest any errant soldier and to lock them up in Curragh Camp. Many the Commanding Officers were extremely busy the following mornings having to hand out many disciplinary awards to their errant soldiers it could be in a form of a fine or indeed a period of imprisonment. At various times in Ireland the Regiment was based in County Clare and there were some members of the Regiment were scattered and based at Ennis, Tulla and Limerick. During one of the Regiments many counter terrorist patrols they were once again deployed on horseback and in their traditional formations carrying out the role of cavalry and not dismounted or deployed as infantry it was a time when the cavalry had been issued with armoured vehicles some of the British Army units were finding out to their cost travelling around the many country roads in trucks and armoured vehicles in Ireland the military vehicles were proving to be extremely restrictive hence the need for mounted cavalry as the cavalry would cover vast tracks of real estate and could also enter wooded copses without having to dismount whereas military vehicles were extremely restricted to only traveling along mettle roads as they certainly could not travel off road. On one occasion Fred and his "mates" were worried that they were becoming too exposed in the open countryside without any natural habitat to protect them or to afford some form of camouflage and concealment the troopers were very concerned about being sat high up and exposed on horseback and making themselves prime targets for any deadly IRA snipers. Many of the IRA's snipers had served and had been discharged from the British Army they were men who had served with the British Army during the great war. One could say they had been trained by the very best. Luckily enough none of Fred's colleagues during their tour of duty had been "taken out" by sniper fire but while they were deployed in the countryside each soldier was alert and acutely aware of the dangers when fighting the insurgents. There was a very sad occasion when the Regiment had been deployed on yet another anti-terrorist patrol deep within the Irish countryside the local IRA Commander had been "tipped off" regarding a British Army Cavalry Regiment having been deployed throughout the local area and it was the Regiment Fred was serving in they had been carrying out many searches they had been looking for arms caches and had been gathering intelligence regarding the local and very active IRA battalion who had been operating in the very same area the cavalry Regiment were currently searching. The Regiment began to cross open ground and they were heading towards a couple of isolated houses the were dotted in and around the Regiments designated search area. Unknown at the time the local IRA had setup a decoy by having deliberately fired a shot into the air from in and around the deserted buildings it had been a clever ploy to draw some of the cavalry towards the buildings and to try and get members of the unit to move along the only mettle road leading to the deserted buildings. The intelligence the local IRA unit had obtained was to lead the commander to believe that there was only a small number of cavalry in the area and the British Army were carrying out searches in the terrorist's operational area they seemed to know the soldiers was a mounted unit and not the usual British armoured units or truck bound infantry. The insurgents had managed to obtain some overhead telephone wire and had stripped the outer protective covering to expose the bare copper wire and they had tied one end of the wire to a telegraph post and ran the wire across a sunken road and proceeded to tie the other end of the wire to a broken farm cart ensuring the wire was stretched tightly across the road and they had made sure it was stretched roughly at the head height of someone who was riding a horse and to the troopers riding their horses everything looked and seemed innocent enough there hadn't been anything suspicious to make the soldiers think otherwise. Three British soldiers on horseback were sent at the canter along the road and following up behind them was a machine gun team it was standard military practice. Whilst the remainder of the Regiment had surrounded the buildings in the hope of trapping anyone who might still be inside the buildings. Fred was sat astride his sturdy mount "George" the unit were by now trotting in open order it would enable them to hopefully capture any terrorists if they had decided to make good their escape it was a very stressful time for all as a rogue experienced IRA sniper could be situated in a concealed position a distance away from where the soldiers were patrolling and a sniper could of so easily have taken a shot at the troopers and possibly kill one or at the most two. Fred thought that it had seemed far too quiet there weren't any children playing outside of the houses and there wasn't any washing pegged on the lines it was a nice windy summers day and it would have been normal practice at that time of the morning for children to have been playing outside and for some washing to have been hanging out to dry but on this morning there wasn't any activity and it had made the Commanding Officer feel very uneasy and the scene before him was making him feel as though something wasn't quite right. The soldiers were used to approaching isolated buildings but the scene before them did not look right at all some were jittery. Something was amiss and most of the soldiers had already opened their rifle holsters just as the second in command gave the order for the troopers to unsling their rifles and to ride at the ready with rifles at the ready Fred thought "this is it the Officers are bloody thinking the same as us troopers something is definitely up" Meanwhile the three troopers had carried on riding along the mettle road everything seemed to be normal apart from the horses hoofs making a racket on the cobbled road as they approached a bend in the road the troopers had decided to ride around the bend in single file but still at a canter. Suddenly the first rider had his hat knocked from his head but sadly the second rider was not so fortunate he had followed behind the first horseman and had seen his hat fly from his head but unfortunately it had been the very last thing he would ever see on this earth. He had been slightly taller than the first horseman and it was at this point as the telephone wire was camouflaged against the morning's bright sky and couldn't be seen against the bright sky and it had sliced through the second troopers neck the force of the wire together with the speed the trooper was riding had added to the efficiency of the makeshift garrote. The wire hadn't quite severed the trooper's head from his spine but at the same time as the wire had garroted the trooper he had made a chilling scream and gurgling sounds the trooper had instinctively grabbed at his throat there was masses of blood spurting from his neck and the blood had gushed from the front of his neck through his fingers. The first rider had turned in his saddle to look back towards where he had heard the noise the sight he saw before him had turned his blood cold the third rider pulled up his mount he had only just missed being garroted himself everything had happened so quickly and both remaining riders had quickly dismounted from their mounts and had rushed over to where their dead comrade was laying in the road it was all far too late he had passed away in such a horrific manner. The dead soldier was laying on a road in the beautiful Irish countryside the country scene around his body was so peaceful but a man, in a beautiful natural scene in the sunny Irish countryside, had met such a terrible death. His blood was flowing everywhere his eyes were open and seemed to be staring in a look of shock as though his eyes couldn't believe what they had witnessed. The road was flowing with his blood it was beginning to dry in the morning sun. The first trooper had cut the wire from the telegraph pole the trooper was bloody angry and he had taken his carbine from its holster and against every rule in the book he placed his carbine in his right shoulder and fired a shot into the air the horses had been trained not to bolt under the sound of gun shots. The horses had begun to move around the trooper's body it did look as though the horses could sense that death was around them. A member of the machine gun team ran towards the troopers and he had his carbine drawn he had been anticipating a terrorist skirmish he heard the single shot ring out also as the shot rang out a Regimental officer had galloped at great speed across the open expanse he had come from the direction of the main element of the Regiment as they were waiting in an open field to descend on the derelict buildings he was galloping towards the sunken road where the troopers on the road were by now extremely distressed at the callous death of their comrade. The officer soon arrived at their location he quickly dismounted from his horse and he had soon realised from the sight of the soldier's body laid out before him on the road he could see there was absolutely nothing more that could be done for the garroted soldier. The troopers who had witnessed his murder had tried to explain to the officer about the circumstances around his death. They were far too excited and extremely angry to make any sense. Fred was sat astride his mount as the shot had rang out and at the time he realised that the shot had been fired somewhere towards the road and not over at the deserted buildings. He could tell by the crack of the shot it had certainly been fired from a rifle and not from a pistol every type of weapon has a very different characteristic sound when a cartridge is fired. Suddenly, the officer sped on his horse and headed towards the roadside at great speed, the RSM had shouted to the remainder "stand still men everything is in hand just keep an eye out for any suspicious movement to your front". Meanwhile at the roadside it had looked obvious to the officer who had been sent to investigate, that the poor trooper had been garroted he would not have known too much about it, he could see that the troopers head was literally hanging onto his torso by some skin and the bones in his neck had been cut through and the scene on the road looked as though a butcher had had a go at his neck with a cleaver. The officer summoned a horse and cart from the quartermaster's department that was with the column the troopers body was soon picked up from the road and it was unceremoniously slung onto the back of the cart the troopers mount was also tied to the rear of the cart. As the cart slowly passed by the soldiers that were still stationed on the road bowed their heads out of respect for the man. The officer ordered the remaining two troopers to carry on down the road with extreme care as they moved towards the buildings at the bottom of the road the machine gun team was to remain in their position and to be ready to open fire on anyone trying to make a run for it and to give covering fire if the two troopers were shot at. Fred and the remainder of the column could see the officer and his horse they were galloping towards the main column at full speed who were still standing in the middle of the field. The returning officer immediately reported to the Commanding Officer and he had quickly briefed him on what he had found on the road. The terrorist group who had carried out the atrocity would be by now long gone from the scene of the crime. The Regiment continued in open column towards the houses Fred and the other troopers didn't need to be told, about the details the officer had reported to the CO, they had known it hadn't been good news. As the horses crossed the open field there hadn't been any movement observed from around the buildings or in the windows of the houses. As the troopers left the field to surround the houses the troopers had dismounted and some of the soldiers had entered the deserted buildings the second in command emerged from one of the houses he had confirmed that the house was empty the RSM came out from another house and he had also confirmed that the house was empty one of the other Sergeant Majors reported to the CO confirming the pigsty was empty and nothing had been hidden in or around the sty. The CO requested that the second in command wrote a note regarding the circumstances surrounding the trooper's untimely death including the abandonment of the houses as the information gathered would help to build a much larger Intelligence picture of the area and the information would add to the intelligence gathering operations within the whole of the county. Fred and the remainder of the troopers knew it had been a very bad day for the Regiment.

Chapter 5 - Reality

By 1926 the Regiment had once again moved to England and this time they had been billeted at Tidworth Barracks in Wiltshire and by the time the Regiment had returned Fred had almost served seven years in the Army and by now he had felt that he had a stomach full of military life. He, had come to a decision it was now time for him to leave the Army and to settle down and to make a life away from the Army environment. His relationship with Sarah had by now grown from strength to strength and he was fast approaching 26 he had felt by making the decision to leave the Army was the right thing for him to do. He had eventually requested his discharge from the Regiment and the Army and in accordance with regulations he had to submit a letter in writing to his Officer Commanding who would have to interview Fred just to ensure that he wasn't making a grave mistake. His OC had informed Fred he would not stand in his way if it was what he really wanted to do? the OC had approved Fred's request and his application had been forwarded to the Commanding Officer, CO. He eventually went in front of the CO who had by then rubber stamped his request for his discharge from the Army. In June 1926 before his discharge he had decided that he was going to stay with his mother Susan and her husband Henry in Hull at the very last moment he had decided that he would settle in Liverpool and within the Dingle area it was very close to where Sarah was living with her parents. He had written to her explaining all about his plans he had an offer that he just could not refuse and the address in Liverpool was submitted along with his discharge papers. As the Regiment was currently based in England he had travelled to Liverpool by train. Travelling by train had enabled him to carry the very few belongings he owned including the many photographs of his service in the Army. Sadly, today only one photograph remains of Fred looking all resplendent in his uniform on his favourite mount George. Fred had to complete his discharge papers prior to leaving the Army included were his Resettlement documents and he had to supply a discharge address so that the War Department could send him any documentation regarding his military service and any monies he may have accrued. He had provided the Army with an address in Isaac Street, Dingle, Liverpool. It was quite ironic because during his military service over in Ireland he had travelled around the Dingle area on many a military mission. He had soon settled down into a new life and he had been very lucky as he had managed to obtain some work as a seaman serving onboard a local fishing vessel. It was during this period in his life he and Sarah had taken their relationship to a higher and a more intense level. She was still extremely reluctant to introduce Fred to her parents, George and Annie; as the situation at home was extremely volatile. Sarah was becoming more and more frustrated with Fred for not having chased up his divorce and for not having submitted the application to start the divorce proceedings in the courts. It was fast approaching 1927 and he had been estranged from his wife May since she had committed adultery way back in 1921. In the July of 1927, he had moved into much more comfortable lodgings in Upper Stanhope Street, Toxteth Park and the fishing job was paying extremely well the fish catches were very profitable and his skipper would push the fishing boat and the crew to the very limits of endurance. There wasn't a single member of the crew who had ever complained because everyone had been reaping the rewards for working so hard by the means of some extra cash. It had not stopped Sarah badgering him to do something about the divorce and at the same time she had, enough of her parent's and tensions at home were running very high and she did not need Fred causing a bigger headache regarding his marriage and his divorce. In her eyes, it was coming up for almost six years since his wife had committed adultery and he should have sorted things out by now. She was so annoyed with his lack of action. By the late 1920's a divorce was still very expensive and nothing had changed since he looked at obtaining a divorce in 1922 Sarah was a very astute women, she knew of a junior solicitor and she had asked him if they could meet up after he had finished work they had arranged to meet up at a coffee house within the city centre and when they had met up she was very direct and asked him about how Fred could go about obtaining a divorce and she had reminded him of his financial circumstances and to the fact that he had no money the solicitor had highlighted the fact that he would have to prove beyond any doubt to the courts and with a very watertight proof of his wife's adultery and she to the fact that she had been cohabitating with another man and if it was possible he would have to provide the name of the other person involved. As to the costs he would have to prove he was so poor and that he would not be able to pay the full solicitors fees and any court costs if he couldn't prove he was poor the legal costs would be very substantial. Sarah thanked her friend for the free advice and left the coffee house she was feeling so sure Fred had already obtained enough evidence to satisfy the court but they need to see the evidence and the details of his wife's adultery. Sarah would have to explain to him whatever he did he was not to disclose his "extra" money to any of the solicitors especially the court personnel. He was to get the skipper to agree to write a letter to the courts outlining Fred's "normal" weekly wage but under no circumstance was he to mention the extra money he was earning on the side. When she visited his lodgings she went through everything her solicitor friend had told her about the court proceedings Fred still had his notebook in his kit bag it was the same notebook he had taken to Hull when he had visited his mum back in 1921 he had written down the date with which May had supposedly committed adultery and he had also written the name of the man she was alleged to have had an affair with including the address he was staying and the details that a neighbour had given regarding the man with who May was cohabiting with and it was the same man. Sarah thought "at last he has done something bloody right surely it would go to helping him with his divorce application". He dug out his notebook and sat by the kitchen table with such a stupid grin on his face Sarah said, "Oh Freddy you are such a bloody stupid sod I do love you, you are such a soft git" he looked at her and replied, "I know". Later, he had obtained the letter from his skipper it had been written in pencil on a scrap piece of paper but it would do the trick he had certified the wages he was paying Fred. He took a day off work and walked the streets of Liverpool trying to find a solicitor who would take on his case it would have to be as a "poor" client and there weren't that many solicitors who would take on such a client. Eventually he found a solicitor to take on his case he had to prove and to swear under oath that he wasn't earning any more than fifty pounds a year and he had to prove that he wasn't earning more than two pounds a week. He also had to produce his skippers letter with a breakdown of his wages he showed the solicitor the skippers letter with a breakdown of his pay and it had proved good enough. On his divorce application, he was officially confirmed and was legally classed as being poor within the eyes of the law. The paper work was duly submitted to the divorce courts and on the 12th of August 1927 the court had finally granted him his divorce. Sarah was over the moon he had finally got his finger out and had filed the divorce paperwork to the courts. That evening they went out to celebrate his long awaited and newly found freedom and in her eyes her life with him was about to start and at last and they had a future to look forward to. For Sarah, her relationship with Fred would pose some major issues with her parents and she knew her father would never agree to her relationship or to Fred or to his marriage proposal. The day soon came when she would have to tell her parents about her relationship and future. It had taken a lot of guts and tremendous bravery on her part to face her parents and more so her father George and she would have to tell them about her future with her Freddy. Her father George was a very hardworking dock labourer and it was very well known within the family that he had an extremely short temper it wouldn't take too much to set him off. Sarah duly went to visit her parents and they didn't live too far away from where she was currently living with Fred. Her mother Annie answered the door she had been wondering just how long it would take before Sarah would come to visit. Annie had already been informed about her daughter living in sin and with a divorcee she had felt embarrassed about the situation she hadn't brought her daughter up to act in this shameful manner. Annie quickly ushered Sarah into the parlour as she didn't want her neighbours to see what was going on her father George was sat in his favourite chair he had a very long face on him Sarah could tell straight away he was ready to blow his top. Sarah sat across from him as her mother walked into the room with a pot of tea Sarah said, "thank you mum" as her mother started to pour the tea from the best tea pot Sarah turned to her father and enquired "how are you dad are you well"? George replied, "how do you bloody think I am"? Sarah thought "well that is so bloody typical of him" her mother said "George, please this is really important to Sarah so please just listen to what she has to say will you" Sarah had a sip of tea and began "Mum dad I have something really important to tell you,

104

well you see I have met the most wonderful man" George immediately reacted "oh for fuck's sake he has got you pregnant hasn't he, you're not bringing another man's bastard into my house" She calmly explained that no one had got her pregnant she had tried her best to explain to her father that her new man was a divorcee and there was no easy way of explaining the situation to her him. George hadn't let her finish what she had wanted to tell him he had already exploded and went into such a rant "there is no bloody way a daughter of mine is seeing a divorcee and that's bloody final do you hear me girl what the hell do you think you are doing you stupid girl" she was well aware her father would react in this way he continued until he finally exploded he was in such a rage Sarah thought to herself, I haven't even got to the best part yet". Annie suddenly piped up "Sarah have you really thought this through sweetheart this is very serious"? She replied "yes mam I have always known that Freddy was the man for me as soon as I first met him when he was on leave from Ireland many years ago" As soon as George heard her latest revelation he again went on the rampage "you fucking what, do you mean to tell me you have been seeing this fucker over many years and not only is he a married man you now mean to tell me you have been having a relationship with the man when you were under bloody age I'll have his bloody guts for fucking garters where is the cradle snatcher now"? She went on to tell him about her lover it was at this point her mother had gone white with fright and she seemed to be totally dumfounded at what Sarah had said including the fact he was 7 years older than she was. He father saw red he just couldn't control himself any more "did you say on leave from bloody Ireland don't fucking tell me he was part of the British Army of occupation this just gets bloody better and better oh girl I just don't believe what you have done to us? I will never give you permission to marry him" and at that point she became defiant and responded to her father "I shall wait until I am 21 then" it was at this point George physically frog marched her from the house and threw her out onto the street it would be the very last time she would ever visit the family home. Annie was in absolute hysterics she was sobbing her heart out but at the same time she knew she could never defy her husband and take her daughters side against his authority. George shouted at Sarah in the street "fuck off you're not wanted here and never set foot across this threshold ever again do you bloody hear me" she was sobbing and she could hear in the distance her mother crying she was almost wailing. Annie knew no one could change her husband's mind especially when his mind had been made up as his word was gospel. As Sarah walked down the street with a feeling of utter disgrace some of the neighbours had opened their front doors to see what all the commotion was about some of the women had stepped onto the pavement with their arms folded nosing at the commotion in the street George saw them and shouted at the women "fuck off and get a bloody life this has nothing to do with you lot, you're just a bloody bunch of bloody nosy cows" and with that he slammed the front door shut. Sarah had known full well how her father was going to react but at the same time she had felt as though a huge burden had suddenly been lifted from her shoulders. She could move on and could get on with living her life with her Freddy. She went to his digs and asked for a very sweet cup of tea and as she sat down he asked her "how did it go sweetheart" she replied it went exactly how I thought it would go Freddy" he replied, "well your mum and dad know everything about us now there is no need to hide as it is all out in the open and it is not such a secret it is now time to get on with our lives and plan for the wedding" she replied, "yes my love". Fred had recently left working on the fishing boat and instead managed to get a job as a tug boatman within the Liverpool docks as it was a much safer job the pay was a bit better than the work fishing out on the dangerous seas. It was the same for everyone working at the time provided he didn't get himself injured there wasn't any employment insurance. Sarah had an ally within her family it was her aunt Elaine she would often visit Sarah and would update her on her parents and how they were getting on. At the same time Annie was aware her sister was in contact with her daughter. Sarah would often go to visit her aunt and they would sometimes meet her mother under very different circumstances at her aunt's lovely and peaceful house. If her father had ever found out there would have been severe repercussions for her mother so it was much better this way as the less George knew about the meetings the better all round. At Fred and Sarah's wedding it had only been her aunt Elaine who had attended from her side of the family. Fred had a relative who lived in Liverpool he had originated from the Faroe Islands and he had attended the wedding. It was a very small Registry wedding not many people had attended. The only positive thing to come out of the wedding was the fact they were now married and were extremely happy it had been tinged with some sadness Sarah had so wished her mother might have been able to attend she had thought it would have been a bloody miracle if both of her parents had of attended but sadly she didn't believe in miracles. On the couple's marriage certificate Fred had falsely informed the Registrar he was a bachelor and it had been very naughty of him as he was a divorcee it was lucky for him no one had informed the Registrar of his false declaration at least he had obtained his divorce from May thank god for small mercies. Life was very tough in the Peterson household and it hadn't been too long before Sarah had fallen pregnant. During the time working on the tugs Fred had received a very nasty injury to his back he would have to leave work and he had ended up working as a lowly paid driver on a horse and cart he had the found work at the Admiralty department in Liverpool the North Atlantic Headquarters moving various stores by horse and cart and life was very tough he had to find enough money to pay the rent etc. Once again Fred would experience another period of deprivation and hardship but this time it would be with a family of his own. Sarah was pregnant with her first child and when their first child Anne was born they had to move out of their one bedroom flat. They soon found themselves living in a 3 bedroomed flat above a post office on Mill Street in the Dingle area it was cheap enough and Fred could just afford the rent they lived from hand to mouth they knew the area very well and had many family and friends living in the area. After moving to the flat It was big enough to live in and if they had any more children they would have the room to accommodate them. Fred was over the moon with the birth of his first child he didn't want any more children as he thought one was enough and their financial situation wasn't the best in the world. It was Sarah who had wished for a large family she had kept her thoughts to herself she didn't want to let Fred know how she felt. Sarah's mother had been informed of the birth of her first grandchild it was her sister Elaine who had broken the news to her she realised the falling out between George and their daughter was ongoing and without any end in sight. She couldn't even dare broach the subject with George for fear of him taking it out on her over the years he still hadn't mellowed he was still very volatile even more so after he'd had a skin full of beer. Soon another daughter would enter the Peterson household and it hadn't been too long after the birth of Anne when Sarah once again fell pregnant with her second child Dorothy. It would mean the family would struggle even more and at the time it was a god send that Fred still had some sort of work as without it the family would have been destitute. At the time, the world was changing and quickly. In Germany, there was a new political party it was increasingly growing in popularity with the people of Germany the party was known as the socialist Party of Germany it was better known as the Nazi Party. It wouldn't be too long before it became the only ruling party in Germany and once it had gained power it would go on to persecute a minority religious group and the group of people were the Jewish population in Germany and eventually they would become persecuted in every country the Nazi's occupied. At the same time, Japan had invaded Manchuria to exploit its vast untold natural resources Japan did not have an abundance of natural resources. Today Manchuria is part of China. For Fred and Sarah, the events unfolding in other parts of the world had no bearing on their lives whatsoever. They didn't even own a wireless and he certainly didn't waste his money on buying newspapers. It was fast approaching 1934 and she had once again fallen pregnant and when she informed Fred of the news he almost fell off his chair he just could not keep up with children popping out. Sarah had told him in the future he was to wear a condom whenever he made love to her. His wages had only just stretched far enough to keep the family financially above water he had thought to himself "my god not another bloody kid", as soon as he had regained his composer he said to Sarah "Sweetheart we are going to have to make even more cut backs if we are going ahead and having this child" Sarah replied "well Freddy you are going to have to stop having a pint or two in the local boozer on a Friday night aren't you? do you hear me?" it was now 1935 and their third baby was born and once again it was another baby girl the baby had been very lucky she was delivered in a local terraced house in Isaac Street her mum was lucky to have a midwife to assist in the delivery of her baby daughter, Chloe, the baby was born into a life of poverty and during the child's early life she would only know of poverty and the hardships. She would only know of a normal life without poverty on the day of her own marriage many years later. Her father Fred once again had found a new job as he had to leave the job with the Admiralty it wasn't paying for his growing family, his back was still playing him up and needs must he needed to find a more skilled job. He once again found work on the river Mersey and this time he got work as a river bargeman and once again he was making good money. The barges would have to be towed by tugs the barges had carried many commodities including grain, coal, sugar, sand and gravel it was extremely hard work and very long hours some of the barges would carry a load of just under three hundred tonnes. In 1939 Great Britain declared war on Germany, Japan and Italy the three countries were widely known as the Axis powers of evil. In 1940 the young Chloe was evacuated to the countryside due to the high possibility of the Liverpool docks being bombed by the German Luftwaffe but the bizarre thing was she was the only one out of all the children in the family to be evacuated. It was only going to be poor little Chloe who was to be evacuated she was only five years old and didn't understand why it was only her who was going to have to leave the family and to an unknown destination and must live with complete strangers. Her mother had told her she was going to live with a nice family in the countryside when young Chloe left Liverpool she was wearing a black duffle style coat, a dress and a pair of second hand shoes. She had a cardboard box with string slung across her shoulder the string was also tied to the box and inside the box was her "gas mask" she had a bag with what could only be described as scraps of clothing she didn't even own any pyjamas or slippers never mind a dressing gown. She looked in such a sordid state Chloe should have reported to her local school but as she had never really attended school her mother had taken her directly to Lime street train station where her mum wished her good luck and with that the steam began to billow smoke from the funnel of the train as it pulled away from the platform it soon left Lime street station. Young Chloe was extremely scared of what was going on around her and what would happen to her she didn't understand what was going on and it was all far too much for her to take it in. It was the very first time she had ever left home never mind travelling on a train to god knows where to and there were more young children who were also being evacuated and they were all travelling by train from Liverpool to a destination somewhere in the countryside. It has been said that almost one hundred and fifty thousand people were evacuated from Liverpool and most of them were children. Travelling with the children was a team of adults from the Liverpool council who were escorting them to ensure the children arrived safely at the various destinations. Chloe was sat in a carriage very much wondering why her siblings hadn't been evacuated with her it was playing on her mind, she was beginning to think she had done something very wrong to her mother. The train eventually arrived at Acton Bridge Railway Station and the station was roughly a mile and half away from her destination in Weaverham Cheshire standing on the platform was a full figure of a lady and a thin man they were there to collect her from the train station and unknown to her she was going to stay with them for the duration of the evacuation however long that was going to be. Her time in Cheshire would be in the lap of the gods the couple who had come to collect her looked upon Chloe with such sadness she had looked in a very sorry and pitiful state the couple had travelled on a horse and cart Chloe giggled when all three of them had stood next to the horse. Just before they climbed on board the cart the couple had introduced themselves to the little scruffy looking girl as Mr and Mrs Jones they knew a little bit about Chloe it had been provided by the social services. Mrs Jones opened her handbag and clenched a sweet into her hand and offered it to Chloe she grabbed the sweet but Mrs Jones said to her "and what do we say", she replied "Yes please Mrs Jones" Mrs Jones replied "that's a good girl manners don't cost anything" she then handed her the sweet she had rarely been given any treats back home at first she thought "I will put the sweet in my coat pocket and save it for later on she thought about it no Mrs Jones has given me the sweet for me to eat now I am sure she must have lots of sweets oh it is going to be so nice here". With that all three of them had disappeared out of the station car park and into the village. From that moment on she knew she was going to be very happy staying with the Jones's it was a late summer's afternoon and the warm sun felt so comforting on young Chloe's skin. The following morning, she came downstairs to the smell of toast in the air and set out on the kitchen table there was a breakfast of toast, butter and marmalade she had never seen the likes of oranges in a jar before and it was the very first time she had ever seen it and there it was a very strange looking substance on the table it was in a magical looking jar the colour of orange marmalade jar had sparkled in the morning sun as it streamed through the kitchen windows. Ma Jones asked Chloe if she wanted some scrambled egg for breakfast she had declined the offer as she was still fascinated by the jar of marmalade with its orange rind floating inside. It was her first breakfast consisting of toast topped off with a huge dollop of marmalade the bread had been cut so thick there was a piece of toast with a large blob of butter melting into the toast she had a large glass of milk to wash it all down with. Ma Jones had proper tumbler glasses to drink from she had watched in fascination as Chloe looked at the glass and began to feel the glass and it was at that point Chloe had asked Ma Jones what was she drinking from she replied, "why it's a glass she replied I haven't seen a proper glass before?" Ma Jones was a little shocked and suddenly a tear began to well up in her eyes the little girl sat before her continued "we only have jam jars at home" she had felt so very sad and so sorry for the little girl who was sat at her kitchen table, she thought "Oh my god you poor child" there was far worse to come Ma Jones was in the bathroom showing Chloe some of the things that she must not touch the little asked her what were the brushes used for? Ma Jones replied "they are toothbrushes, you have to put some tooth paste on the brush and then you clean your teeth with them" she said "oh no we use soot and salt on our fingers back home not silly brushes and funny paste" Mrs Jones then had shown her how to clean her teeth properly with one of the tooth brush Ma Jones thought "what sort of home has the child come from" After breakfast she took Chloe to the local school and spoke to the head teacher about the little girls situation she had packed a lunch for her and had left her with the head teacher and she had soon made young Chloe feel at home. After school Chloe was so happy she had skipped back to Ma Jones's house the house was only a few hundred yards from the school. She told Mrs Jones that she had loved her first day at school and the head teacher had given her a note for Mr and Mrs Jones to read and in the letter the head teacher had explained that young Chloe could not read or write and so the teacher's would have to give her some extra lessons to enable her to catch up with the other children bearing in mind it was only an infant's school she had also pointed out that Chloe was a cheeky little girl but not in a nasty way she had only attended the school for just a day and already she was regaling her classmates with stories of her life in Liverpool and some of the stories had been let's just say at the least very imaginative. The Jones house was in a rural part of Chester behind the house was a wood it was where Chloe and her newly found friends would play for hours. The Jones also had a small holding at the bottom of the garden it housed some chickens and most of the back garden had been taken up with growing vegetables. The front garden was swamped in a carpet of flowers in so many different colours. She had been taught to pick up and handle the chickens and to help Ma Jones to collect the fresh eggs that were freshly laid each morning all the food she ate was so fresh and most of the vegetables would come straight from Mr Jones's allotment. He had worked as a farm labourer and the farmer would often give him various cuts of meat from the farm animals as soon as the animals had been slaughtered and Ma Jones worked in a munitions factory but she never once neglected Chloe besides the Jones's had an older daughter who had also lived at the house along with Ma Jones's mother sadly her mother had suffered a stroke and she would sit in a rocking chair Chloe would think the old lady had slept all night in the rocking chair. To her life was fantastic she had hardly known her father "Freddy" who had to work all hours of the day just to put a roof over the families' head and a little food on the table and after that there wasn't much left over and it only paid for the very basics from his meagre wages. Back at the house in Cheshire Chloe loved getting out of her bed and each morning she was always eager to get off to school and during the period of her evacuation she had felt for the very first time ever that she had felt so loved and was wanted. She had inherited her dad's dry sense of humour she was extremely sarcastic and it was going to haunt her in later life. For Chloe, it was such a blissful life living with the Jones's family. One evening the War had suddenly reared its ugly head and had interrupted her tranquil and peaceful world. That evening most of the village had been disturbed by the sound of Aircraft flying high above the village everyone in the Jones household were standing in the rear garden looking skyward and ready to get into the air raid shelter Mr Jones had built the air raid shelter in the garden and as they stood looking up at the sky no one could make out the aircraft they were flying overhead they could certainly hear the sounds of the aircraft engines and it was while everyone was watching the skies Chloe overheard Mr Jones say to Ma Jones, "bloody hell Ma I wouldn't like to be in Liverpool tonight when that lot arrive and drop their bombs I think the poor sods are in for a torrid night" and Ma Jones replied "yes poor buggers" Chloe looked up at Mr Jones and said "will our mam and dad be OK Mrs Jones" Ma Jones had reassured her the best she could and she said "everything would be fine sweetheart". One day totally out of the blue Mr Jones had received a letter from the Liverpool social services department informing them of Chloe's father "Freddy" having recently passed away in very difficult circumstances after a long illness at the time of his death in the letter there hadn't been any mention of Chloe having to return home to Liverpool or even a letter from her mum it had been left to the authorities in Liverpool to inform the Jones family they were the only people to write to them explaining about the death of Chloe's father. A soon as Chloe had returned from school Mr Jones sat her down and had tried very hard to explain the best way he could about the news of her father having passed away she hadn't shown any emotion to the sad news of her father's death she had hardly known her father and she was approaching five when she had been evacuated. She had faintly remembered a tall man who was stood next to her mother when her mother was pregnant with her brother Peter. After Mr Jones had explained things to her she looked at Mr Jones and said it that it? can I go out to play now please? In Cheshire Chloe was living in what in her eyes was a paradise it had felt pure bliss she had never been so happy in her life over time she hardly knew what mother looked like Chloe was a nice cheeky child without any menace she would happily play for hours with her friends in the air raid shelters in the gardens. A year later a social worker from Northwich arrived at the Jones household it was on a Saturday morning and Chloe was where she always went and it was out playing in the local woods with all her friends. Mr Jones answered the door and a man was standing at the door he knew as soon as he had clapped eyes on the man who was standing at his front door the man looked very official if anyone can look official he did he knew it had to be something to do with Chloe, Ma Jones shouted "who is it George" she was in the kitchen and George had stepped into the kitchen with the visitor, Ma Jones said "oh no please don't take her away" the man said "I am so very sorry Mrs Jones but the little girl's mother has approached the social services department in Liverpool and she is wanting her daughter to come back home where she rightfully belongs" Ma Jones said "but her mother has never been in contact with the dear child in all the years she has been living with us her mother has never once bothered to visit her since she was evacuated we have had our recent application to adopt Chloe rejected, her mother doesn't want to know her own daughter I just don't know why she is bothering at this stage in the little girl's life, she is so settled here", Mr Jones turned to his wife and said "Julie we knew this would happen one day sweetheart" Julie replied "I know we did George but it's just not fair on us or poor Chloe she will be devastated at the news". The man had left the house and had told them he would be back in a fortnight just as soon as he had contacted the Liverpool social services department and of course the little girl's mother. Chloe came back from playing outside and as she walked into the house she knew that there was something terribly wrong, poor Ma Jones she was sat at the kitchen table and in tears Mr Jones had tried so very hard to explain the situation to her and about what had just happened and the hardest part was trying to tell her she would have to return to her mother in Liverpool and Chloe shouted at Mr Jones "No Mr Jones please I don't want to go back there please don't let them send me back it's horrible there". Chloe had been staying at the Jones's for five years now and she was ten years old now Ma Jones said, "sweetheart we are not your parents I am afraid your mum really wants you to come back home" Chloe said, "my home is here with you" and with that she went to her bedroom and that evening she cried herself asleep and in her eyes the news was her worst nightmare and her idyllic life was about to change and it would not get back on track for another 11 years or so. The remaining fortnight flew by and it was now 1945. The war had ended and more importantly for Chloe she was going to have to go and live with her mother it was a cynical ploy on behalf of her mother the only reason that her mother had wanted her to come back home was because in the June of the same year the government of the day had introduced the new families allowance and the state would provide payments to those families who had children and when "Freddy" had passed away in the November of 1943 he had died of pneumonia and he had died such a painful and pitiful death the National Health Service hadn't been created yet and he had died such a horrible death and during the January of the same year Fred's brother Edwin had also sadly passed away he was only aged 33 Susan had lost both of her sons in the same year and she was present at Edwin's passing he had died at home in Greek street Hull Sarah hadn't yet informed Susan of Fred's death she had only found out about his death many years later Fred hadn't left any financial support or any provision for Sarah and the children but having Chloe back home Sarah would be able to claim the new family allowance of five shillings a month for all 4 children. It meant that she could have some extra money by

117

claiming child allowance not that the money was spent on any of the children. If the new family allowance payments hadn't come into force there was no doubt that young Chloe would have stayed in Cheshire and would have been brought up by Mr and Mrs Jones. War is such a cruel business not only for the combatants it also affects those left at home as much. The Jones's were at the train station along with the local social worker as she had boarded the train for Liverpool. Mrs Jones was deeply upset by the recent events she had dearly cared for young Chloe as though she was one of her own children. Chloe held onto those fond and very happy loving memories when she was living with Mr and Mrs Jones during her evacuation. She would fondly reminisce about her time living in Weaverham to her sons.

Chapter 6 - Home

It had been arranged in advance for Chloe to be met at Liverpool
Lime Street station by her mother and her elder sister Anne. As
the train began to pull away out of Acton Bridge Railway Station
there had been so many tears shed by Ma Jones and of course
young Chloe. As she sat in the carriage all on her own she had felt
once again alone she began to shake with fear as she hadn't a clue
of what life was about to bring her back home she knew that it
would never be a patch on her life while she stayed at
Weaverham she knew that her life had been bad enough when
her father was alive living at home before she had been
evacuated. It had suddenly dawned on her she didn't know what
her mum looked like and as she sat in the carriage she began to
worry about how she would know her once she had arrived in
Liverpool. She was so fearful and full of fear and trepidation at
the thought of meeting her mother once again after such a long
time away. As the train pulled into Lime Street station she
opened the carriage door and stepped onto the platform she was
holding onto her precious suitcase with an iron grip the suitcase
was full of her nice clothes and a few of her lovely toys as she
stood on the platform she had felt a cold icy wind blowing along
the platform and in the distance, she could see a small wiry dark
haired along with an older girl they were walking towards her.
The woman had approached her and said, "are you my Chloe?"
she replied to the stranger standing in front of her "yes and you
must be our mam" the older girl said, "Hello Chloe welcome back
home I am your sister Anne" and with that the three of them
walked out of the very smoky train station her mother hadn't
even hugged her or gave her a kiss it seemed all so cold and

detached there was no love shown towards her by her mother. As they walked towards Mill Street during the walk no one talked and she hadn't liked the look of the built up city centre and in her eyes it looked very dark and grey she had been used to the wide open spaces of the countryside and the freedom to be able to run in to the nearby woods it had only been two days ago since she had been running in the fields outside in the fresh air to her it had been pure heaven and as the three of them walked through the city centre towards the docks area she could see much of the damage which had been caused by the many German air raids on the city the damage hadn't yet been repaired or re-built. Chloe hadn't a clue as to where they were heading to as she didn't know where her family were living she could only just remember the flat they once lived in prior to her evacuation some five years earlier it had been such a long time ago. All three soon arrived at a dingy looking post office in Mill Street they had to walk along a side alley and it smelt of urine and some other very nasty smells they had to climb some steps leading to a dingy flat above a post office the flat was dark and bleak and as soon as Chloe walked inside the flat it had felt very cold and there was a distinct smell of dampness and mold. Her other sister Dorothy was making a pot of tea their mum had placed some empty jam jars on the kitchen table and Chloe looked at the jam jars in such disbelief things hadn't progressed since she had left home almost five years previously it had been such a shock to the system she said "what are these for?" her mother scolded her and said "oh so we have become stuck up have we? look girls we have a bloody posh cow in our midst these, young lady are what you will be drinking from or are they too good for you" she replied "Ma Jones had proper cups to drink from not jam jars, jam jars are for jam and marmalade not for drinking tea from" Her mother once again scolded her and shouted "well you are fucking living here now and in your proper home where you belong" she knew immediately her life would never be the same again. She would never forget Mr and Mrs Jones her mother could never take her fond memories away. Her mother looked at her youngest daughter and callously said "you do know your dad has passed away while you were away living the life of luxury kid" Chloe just couldn't believe how cold, heartless and callous her mother was towards her and she couldn't believe the cold woman who was sat in front of her at the kitchen table was in fact her own mother if it hadn't been for her elder sisters the woman sat in front of her might as well have been a total stranger. She looked around the kitchen and especially at the windows they had some sacking strung up for curtains the whole place looked a mess it looked awful as there wasn't any natural light flooding into the kitchen and her thoughts once again drifted towards the Jones's kitchen with so much sun shining through the kitchen windows and bathing the house in so much natural sunlight. To Chloe the place she was sitting in was a totally different world from where she had been living at over the last five years and it was a living nightmare a very bad dream. Chloe was told she would have to share a bedroom with her middle sister Dorothy she showed Chloe inside what would be her bedroom. As Dorothy opened the bedroom door Chloe suddenly reeled back in horror and froze in the doorway the bed was an old and rickety thing it had seen better days there were wooden slats attached to the main bed frame with six inch nails and there wasn't a mattress anywhere to be seen. Chloe had asked Dorothy "where is the mattress and the sheets I can't see any blankets?" Dorothy laughed at her "wow you must have been living like a princess where ever you were living in Cheshire you have obviously been very spoilt welcome to the real world little sister and you will have to get used to sleeping on the bed slats and being covered in sacking and various old coats". That night Chloe couldn't sleep and she had whimpered whenever she thought back to her time at the Jones's the lovely spanking clean and the pretty house where tons of love and kindness had been showered upon her. Chloe had suddenly realised she had returned to a life of poverty with a such a huge bump they were memories of her past life living with her mother they began to seep back into her memory and they were memories she had blanked from her mind. The following morning, she expected to be sent to a local school as she had done at Ma Jones's. there was no sign that she was going to go to school she had thought oh its ok as I do feel a little tired perhaps our mum had thought I might need an extra day to rest up due to the journey and the excitement of coming back home. Dorothy and Anne were up and dressed for school all of sudden, a little boy came waltzing into the kitchen and at first, she hadn't known who he was but then she had realized he was her younger brother Peter and when he saw her he didn't say very much until their mother came into the kitchen she had explained to her Peter had been born just as she had been evacuated she didn't even know she had a brother. For breakfast Anne had cooked a sticky mess she had tried her best to explain to Chloe that it was porridge Chloe asked her mother "when am I going to school" and she replied, "when I bloody say so and not you ok" Dorothy told her mum to stop swearing. Sarah was stood at the kitchen sink she had lit a cigarette after she finished her cigarette she told Chloe to bring the suitcase to her the one she had brought with her from Cheshire. She walked into the kitchen she had done as she was and had dragged the suitcase to her mother who opened the suitcase and very soon had begun to rummage through the contents and she came across the toys including the nice clothes and she said to Chloe "after your breakfast bring your suitcase with you as we are going to sell everything in the suitcase". After breakfast Chloe struggled to lift the suitcase and she had to practically drag it along the cobbled streets towards a pawn shop. The pair had soon arrived at a local pawn brokers shop her mother had used the shop on lots of occasions when they entered the shop her mother and the shop owner began to rummage through the many goodies contained in the suitcase and the shopkeeper said "yes these are very nice items Sarah and the suitcase is made of very good materials I shall give you a fair price for the whole lot" she replied "I thought so" she took the cash and pocketed the money as mother and daughter walked home they headed towards the flat and Chloe said to her mum "mam why couldn't I have kept my nice things"? her mother replied "shut up whining you don't need those things anymore so just shut your mouth and don't bloody answer me back I don't want to hear any more of your cheek" Chloe replied "no stop it you can't tell me to shut up" her mother virtually spat at her and said "you are just like your bloody father he would always answer me back he was just as cheeky as you are you're just like him".. Schooling wasn't going to be a top priority in Chloe's life any more as her mother had other plans for her. Over the following years young Chloe became feral she didn't attend school much there were many truant officers in the area because truancy was rife and eventually Chloe's mother had again been summoned to the local truancy board and as on so many occasions it became the norm for Sarah to be excused from keeping her daughter away from school only because she had always used the same excuse that she was a widower and would always blame her youngest daughter for skipping off school. Chloe would have dearly loved to have attended school the sad thing was the longer that she stayed away from school the more her education suffered. On the few days that she had attended school the more difficult it became for her to catch up with the remainder of the class she was continuously being punished by the teachers she had struggled during her lessons and Chloe's suffering didn't end there. The children at school were being very cruel towards her she was being bullied it was all due to her lack of education. She could certainly look after herself, as her own mother hadn't looked after her it was always up to Chloe to stand up for herself she had soon learnt to stand on her own two feet this attitude had led her to have many fights and at home her mother was no help as she was also being abused by her in Chloe's life there was so much disruption and chaos. It wasn't a nice period during her upbringing, due to the disruption at school and at home it was leading to her world moving towards a very steep downhill spiral and possibly into an abyss a black hole. Her mother was noticeably different towards her two older children and the boy peter. Dorothy had managed to successfully pass her eleven plus and had gone on to attend a local gramma school, Anne was passing also passing her school exams with flying colours and Peter was doing very well at his school but for poor Chloe it was a totally different story she was rapidly sliding down the educational ladder. Chloe's life was terrible and she was desperately uncared for by her mother. She would do anything her mother would ask of her as she was desperate to feel wanted by her mother and for her to show some love or affection towards her but alas it was never forth coming. Her mother knew exactly how she was treating her youngest daughter it became so obvious to everyone around her. Whenever she wasn't attending school her mother would pack her off outside to obtain certain items for her. Poor Chloe she had only wanted to impress her mother and for her mother to be pleased with her and to reward her with love and affection and she hadn't wanted a lot from her mother. She was often used by her mother to beg and plead for food and on one occasion her mother wrote a note for her to take to the local baker she was able to read parts of the note but alas not everything that had been written on the piece of paper when she eventually walked into the bakery she handed the baker the note he immediately handed her a loaf of bread poor Chloe it was so cold outside she was extremely hungry and as she walked home she had managed to dig a hole into the loaf of bread and was able to dig out pieces of the loaf she ate the bread and it had tasted just like heaven the loaf was still warm it had tasted so fresh and if she had of carried on picking at the loaf she could have so easily have eaten the whole loaf. When she arrived home her mother was hoping mad she couldn't but help notice the large hole in the bread she had ran for it as soon as she had seen her mum pick up a knife and threw it at her but luckily the knife had missed her and instead hit a wall. After the violent incident Chloe had decided to stay away from the flat as she was so scared of going back home she had stayed out most of the evening until her sister Anne had found her and took her back home. When they had arrived home their mother wasn't in it hadn't been a big surprise to the girls. Chloe asked Dorothy "where is our mam then" she replied, "she is out for the night" and they sat down and ate some gruel and went off to bed and the next morning their mother was sat in the kitchen she was fully dressed and she was still wearing the same clothes as she had on the previous evening she was sat in the kitchen smoking a cigarette. She was singing and smoking a player's cigarette Chloe hadn't seen her mother in such a good mood before it was unnerving. Their mother said, "right everyone get yourselves ready for school, not you Chloe you are far too ill to go to school" she replied, "am I, that's news to me" her mum shouted, "shut your fucking mouth girl before you say something you will regret" she hated her mother for shouting and swearing at her in that way she had felt so awful. The others had by this time gone

125

off to school Sarah decided to send her daughter to the bookies with some money and a note and as Chloe walked into the bookies she could see there were a few men inside and she could also hear the sound of a wireless and a commentator was announcing a running commentary during a horse race as she looked around the bookies she could see a man who was stood behind the counter he soon noticed her and shouted "oi no kids in here now bugger off kid" she quickly handed him the note from her mother and he snatched the note out of her hand and he began to read it and said "ok brat give me some money" he took the money and handed her a ticket in return. Chloe arrived back home and gave her mother some change along with the betting slip. Her mother was sat at a kitchen table with a racing newspaper open and was writing out the odds for the next day's horse meeting. Many years later Chloe was by then married and had a child of her own and had popped into the same bookies shop to see the same man was still working at the shop he had immediately recognised her and said "I know you don't I ?" she replied "yes you do" he said "I am so glad you have managed to get away from your mother and by the look of things you are making something of your life" Chloe felt so proud and left to visit her mother in law, Dorothy with whom she had been staying with. As a child Chloe had been so used to doing her mother's dirty work it had been so rare for any of her other siblings to carry out their mother's dirty work. As she became older and wiser she would notice her mother often leaving the flat clutching a book very tightly in her hand she would enter another Post Office just down the road from the flat and after a short while she would come back and would have lots of money. What she hadn't realised was her mother was collecting the family allowance for all four of the children and she also collected her widows pension. Chloe knew that her mother would spend the evening she had collected the allowances she would spend it in the local pubs enjoying herself and seemingly having a very good time and she would return sometime later in the evening to the flat her mother would sometimes bring someone back with her it would normally be a girlfriend. This was different to the nights when the children wouldn't hear her return from her many nights out and more than likely leaving the children to fend for themselves all night and by the following morning she would be sat in the kitchen smoking a cigarette and she would always return before the children had woke each time their mother would be sat wearing the same clothes she had been seen wearing the night before. Once Chloe had been sent outside by her mother in the pouring rain to visit her grandparent's as they only lived a few streets away and as usual her mother was desperately short of money Chloe had managed to find her grandparent's house and she was standing at the front door she banged as hard as she could onto the wooden door and in doing so she had hurt her bony fist. Her mother had told her not to leave her grandparents' house until she had obtained at least sixpence her mother was sure her father George was out of the house and working down at the docks it would leave her mother Annie in the house and would surely answer the door and would surely give her granddaughter the sixpence. Poor young Chloe she had never seen her grandparents even though they only lived a few streets away. The door opened and it was her grandfather George who had opened the door and as he looked down at the tiny weedy and scruffy looking girl stood before him he said "what do you want kid" Chloe innocently told him her mam had sent her to collect sixpence and once again he looked down at Chloe and bellowed "you're a bloody Peterson, now just fuck off and don't ever come back here again do you hear me kid" Chloe looked at him and said "bugger off mister" and began to run down the same street that her mum had walked along some twenty years previously and she was never to return it had seemed as though history had repeated itself. George still hadn't forgiven his daughter for the shame she had brought upon his family he was now taking out his anger on his own granddaughter. When she eventually arrived home and empty handed her mother had taken out her frustration on her but before arriving home Chloe had known full well her mum would blame her for not returning with the money and as she had walked the streets prior to coming home she had noticed there were some boys who were playing pigeon toss it is a street game players take it in turns to throw a coin against a wall and the coin which lands closest to the wall is the winner and the winning thrower takes the other player's coins. Once again her mother had scolded her and so Chloe had stormed out of the flat and as she did so she could hear her mum shout "and don't fucking come back you frigging brat" she ran to where she had last seen the boys playing the game and once again she wanted so much to make amends to her mother for not bringing any money home for her and she soon arrived at the same street she could see the young boys still playing pigeon toss and she ran as quickly as she could to where they were playing some of the boys had piles of pennies stacked up on the ground there were some pennies very close to the wall so she ran over to the boys and pushed them to the ground and grabbed as many pennies as she could and ran as fast as her legs could carry her all the way home. When she arrived home she was so excited and poured all of the pennies onto the kitchen table her mother said, "if you bloody get caught you're on your own girl, do you hear me I don't want to be associated with what you have just done do you hear me brat she then enquired was there were any more pennies left behind"? she replied, "yes mam but I couldn't grab all of the money and besides you said you only needed six pence" her mother slapped her around the face and shouted, "next fucking time don't come back until you have all of the money do you hear me brat and don't come back until you do" she replied, "yes mam". It seemed to Chloe it didn't matter whatever she had done to please her mother it still wasn't enough. Over time her mother taught her to say very bad and nasty things to other people she would put her up so many bad things, some of the things a child of her age should never have been exposed to and her mother would never admit to what she was putting her daughter through. At one of Chloe's schools the headmistress was about to ban her from the school because of her cheek it had been thoroughly encouraged by her mother and once again she was trying hard to please her mum and she wasn't bothered about what others had thought about her. she would never blame her mother for any of her misdemeanours even though it was she who was the chief instigator and had encouraged her to be cheeky and of course her daughter would carry out her mother's instructions to the very letter. It was obvious to others she was extremely loyal towards her mother and she had tried her hardest to please he no matter what it took nor the consequences of her actions. Sometimes her mother would suddenly explode into a fit of rage for no apparent reason and shout "you fucking sod you have brought nothing but trouble and bad luck to me" Chloe replied "why did you bring me back from Ma Jones then" Her mother frequently threw various things at her and on some occasions the objects had hit her and marked her skin there was an occasion where her mother grabbed her around the throat and choked her she had felt she was about to feint it was at this point her sister Anne walked into the room and quickly stepped in and pulled her mother off her. She had managed to stop her from strangling Chloe. Anne said to her mother "get off Chloe and right now and bloody stop it do you hear me, this has to stop" it had been at this point Chloe had finally realised she had been the only child in the family who was being abused by their mother as no one else in the family had been attacked either physically or mentally by her. One year and out of the blue on her birthday Chloe received a package from Ma Jones. Inside the package there was a beautiful bracelet and as she looked at it her mother was hovering around her she was looking at the bracelet she was showing too much interest in the bracelet and Chloe said, "look mum, look at what Ma Jones has sent me for my birthday, it's beautiful isn't it?" her mother replied, "yes Chloe it is very nice". The next morning Chloe couldn't find the bracelet it wasn't anywhere in the flat it had suddenly disappeared and to her horror she had realised her mother was nowhere to be seen over breakfast Chloe had mentioned the loss of the bracelet to her sisters and Anne, said "you won't be seeing that again she will have pawned it by now". The strange thing about their mother was she had herself a little job on the side it had entailed the cleaning of the post office under the flat she hadn't necessarily got on with the post mistress and the cleaning was doing a job of work she was being paid for doing it by the owners of the post office and not by the post mistress. Chloe had attended The Mathew Arnold school when she wasn't playing truant. The truant officers who investigated the various reasons why some children hadn't attended school would frequently visit the flat and they would interview her mother regarding Chloe's frequent truancy. It was soon time for Chloe to join her next school in Northumberland Street. The truant officers knew all about Sarah as they would do considering the number of times they had to visit Sarah regarding Chloe's lack of school attendance and the three sisters would often wonder why there hadn't been any further action taken against their mother for keeping her off school. Whenever Chloe "bunked" off school she had been "employed" by her mother to run messages for instance taking her mother's betting slips to the local bookies and whenever her mum's horses didn't do well she would shout at Chloe and blame her. She would often say things like "it's all your fucking fault that's why I have lost my money it's because you look so bloody miserable whenever you go to place my bets" everything that went wrong with her mother Chloe would end up bearing the brunt of her mother's anger. Rationing in the United Kingdom would not end until 1954 it had been fourteen years after the end of world war two. Her mother would often sell the families ration cards on the black market and as soon as she had successfully sold the cards she would write a note for Chloe to take to the main Rationing Office in Liverpool. Her mother would apply for replacement ration cards contained within the note she would try to explain how she had either lost the cards or they had been stolen she would add she wasn't able to attend the office in person as she had found herself bed ridden due to some sort of illness hence why her young daughter was at the office on her behalf. The letter would sometimes do the trick and new ration cards would duly be issued and without any questions being asked or any further investigation by the civil servants. Growing up Chloe hadn't told a soul about how wicked and abusive her mother had been towards her. Her mother would milk the system dry she would also play on the fact she was a young widow and was finding it desperately hard bringing up four young children on her own. Chloe's truancy would soon catch up with her and so it was as one day Chloe and her mother would have to attend a truancy court hearing all due to Chloe's continuing truancy. In the court, her mother very quickly turned on the water works and the tears were streaming down her face and her daughters Dorothy and Anne were in attendance as so called "witnesses" and the were there to provide moral support to their mother? The proceedings were, a little bit of a farce as it wasn't viable for the court to award her a fine as she was a virtual pauper and so Sarah was given a severe warning. That was that, once again there hadn't been any follow up action and for a while no more checks were carried out by the truancy officers. Chloe had wondered why it was? Chloe's mother suggested to her that she go out and steal a piece of jewellery so her mother could give it to Anne as a birthday present poor Chloe she got caught stealing the cheap bracelet. She had to attend the local magistrates court and once again her mother pleaded with the court to not to send her youngest daughter away and once again she reeled out the many sob stories and had pleaded with the court and had explained her life was so very tough for all the family and it would break everyone's hearts if Chloe was sent to a young offender's home. Chloe's sisters Anne and Dorothy had never missed a day's schooling both were very happy attending school. But Chloe hadn't been given a choice or a chance by her mother to attend school and she was suffering due to the lack of education. Each Wednesday after her court appearance Chloe would have to report to the court office she also had to report that she hadn't been up to any more mischief the local police officers also knew of Chloe's misdemeanor and they would have to report her to the court if in the future she stepped out of line. Her card had well and truly been marked and whenever she had reported to the court office she would have to write out lines in an old exercise book but there was a major problem she couldn't write and so the punishment had been pointless. Due to her mother's fallout with the post mistress in the post office beneath the flat Sarah had to find another post office to cash her benefit's money, luckily enough she had managed to find a post office only a ten minute walk from the flat, Chloe could not understand why she had to do it because she worked as a cleaner in the post office below the flat. Unless it was a very personal falling out? Anne and Dorothy always seemed to be dressed so much better than Chloe as her shoes were always second hand and if they had been too small for her feet to fit in she would have to walk on the backs of the shoes until the backs had broken her shoes would always have so many holes in them which in turn would allow water to seep into the inside of the shoe her feet were constantly soaking wet and very cold. Her mother seemed to deliberately keep her looking scruffy and looking just like a street urchin. She had known no different as she grew older she had noticed the differences between her and her siblings it became so blatantly obvious even her younger brother Peter would be dressed much better than her she started to think that her mother had deliberately dressed her in that manner Chloe began to think was it possible her mother did it so that it would help to get other people to feel sorry for her as Chloe was a huge asset to her mother whenever she sent her out to beg or to con other people. The family had to move to another house in Clive Street, and once again her mother would keep her from attending school and whenever she was off school her mother would have her scrubbing the floors in the house and on many an occasion she would see a man talking to her mother as she beavered away such as scrubbing the floors in the flat and on one occasion the man laughed at Chloe as she had struggled to carry a bucket of water the bucket was full of holes and when the water started to pour out of the holes he thought it was so funny seeing her struggle. One day, her mother was standing outside of the flat she had noticed some teenage boys playing cards she told Chloe to pour water over the lads where they were sat playing cards she duly did what she was told and had poured the water from an upper window over the boys and there had been a lot of colourful language used it had turned the air blue and it was directed towards Chloe. Her mother had told her it was bad luck having people playing cards outside of the house? On an even more darker note her mother would often have men beat up other men the men who had been beaten up were the same men her mother had fallen out with. She knew her mother had a very vicious streak in her and she knew very well as she was frequently on the receiving end of most it. Most nights one of the men who had carried out the beatings on the mother's say so would often stand outside the flat he was the only one she had never invited into the flat it hadn't meant that he had never entered the flat it just meant the girls had never seen him in the flat. They had seen other men visit but he more than likely had visited Sarah when the children weren't around or in bed. Whenever the man stood outside the house Sarah would go outside and join him and they would talk for hours they would stand outside talking and smoking lots of cigarettes. Chloe hadn't trusted the man she would stare outside from her bedroom window she would watch him standing outside with her mum. The same man would continue to visit Sarah even when Chloe had grown into a young woman she had never trusted him. To anyone who knew Sarah she could come across as a very nice person because as a young widow she was gallantry struggling to bring up four children all on her own. There was another person who would frequently visit Sarah and he was the local beat police officer, Bizzie (policeman) it was such a bizarre situation. His mother had owned a local greengrocer by now Chloe was 13 and she had recognised him as the local policeman as she had seen him whenever he walked his beat. On occasions, she would have to take notes written by her mother and the notes were meant for the policeman only she would have to deliver the notes to his mother's shop. Sarah would often say "its bloody bad luck having a copper visit the house" and yet at some time she must have been entertaining the policeman in her bed? She was such a hypocrite as mentioned Sarah would often go out at night and the children would have to fend for themselves. There was never any food on the table it was one of the reasons why children enjoyed going to school because they got to eat a hot school lunch. Chloe hadn't attended school and hence she soon became malnourished. Her mother would throw her out in all kind of weathers be it rain snow or out in the howling winds that would sweep off from the river Mersey and sometimes she was sent out in the rain to go to the local coal yard she would have to queue up in the pouring rain and pay for a sack of coal and drag it all the way back home where her mother would scowl at her for being late her mother would complain that she was freezing and had to do without a fire until the coal arrived. Chloe was often soaked through to the skin there were never any towels to dry herself off with and so she would find dry sacking from a bag of potatoes and she would try to dry herself as best she could. The family had an outside toilet it wasn't one of those shared with other families in the street. They didn't have a bath with running water all they had was a tin bath and the whole family would share the same bath water many a time the girls would visit the various bathing houses dotted around the city. On One rare occasion at school Chloe had to sit a basic test and one of the questions asked was what is the difference between an apple and an orange and her answer was they are both round and one is green and one is orange. At home, she had never eaten an apple or orange but she had vaguely remembered having apples at Ma Jones's house but that was over seven years ago and it was a very distant memory. her mother had once again found herself pregnant this time it was the local policeman's baby hence why Chloe had found herself having to take notes on behalf of her mother to the local grocer's shop at the time he was living with his mother above the shop it was to be the first of many letters she was to deliver the very first note had informed the policeman Sarah had found herself pregnant and the baby was his and informed him that he would have to accept his responsibilities towards her and the baby. The policeman had to be extremely careful that the sergeant at his police station didn't get wind of what had been going on between himself and Sarah especially when he was meant to be on duty but instead he had been visiting Sarah's flat during the night shift what he had done was obviously against all police regulations one regulation was abandoning his beat to visit a woman whilst still on duty. It transpires the policeman and Sarah were to marry but not one of Sarah's children knew what was going on and it was soon obvious their mother was pregnant Anne the eldest child had some idea of what was happening because of the comings and goings between her mother and the policeman and there was the local gossip which was doing the rounds regarding the situation between Sarah and the policeman. The policeman's mother had known a little about what was going on and she had been extremely skeptical about the situation his son had supposedly got himself in to. Sarah was well known within the area and had a bit of a reputation. Behind everyone's back Sarah and the policeman were planning to get married not even his mother knew of his plans if she had he knew she would have put a stop to it all. The policeman had arranged everything including the Registry Office and the wedding reception. The reception was to be held in the rear room of one of the many pubs in the area the landlord had known the groom was a policeman but his money was good the landlord did not want to advertise the fact that the pub was hosting a wedding reception for the local police force, the buffet had been booked and was paid for well in advance. The policeman had one or two of his friends from his police station in attendance. Sarah being Sarah

The Journey

hadn't turned up at the Registry Office the policeman was absolutely devastated as he had to cancel everything he had been extremely embarrassed and distraught at having been stood up at his own wedding. The embarrassment of having been stood up at one's own marriage would hurt anyone and he was absolutely devastated he was so angry just as guests were leaving the Registry Office the policeman's mother turned to him and said "now sort this out you bloody soft lad, I wouldn't be surprised if that bloody woman knows the baby isn't yours and it is in fact another man's child she has been taking you for a bloody ride and a bloody fool" He knew Sarah had humiliated him in front of his family and friends he just didn't know the reason why she had done this to him unless his mum was right and that the baby wasn't his. It wasn't too long after he had been stood up when a friend of Sarah's informed him Sarah had recently given birth to a little baby girl but she had arranged for the baby to be put up for adoption this news was the very last straw and as soon as he had finished his shift that evening he went around to Sarah's flat to have things out with her as it had been so long overdue for days he had been at his wits end never mind at having been embarrassed at the so called wedding of the year and now she going to get rid of his baby just like buying a sack of potatoes he wouldn't be surprised if she had sold the baby as he was now starting to believe everything other people had told him regarding Sarah. He soon arrived at the dingy flat and inside the children could hear a loud knock at the door and then they heard a man shouting and demanding to be let in. Dorothy had opened the door the man stormed into the flat and as he entered the kitchen the children knew it was the policeman and the children had the sense to immediately leave the room and the policeman approached Sarah who by now was sitting at the kitchen table and he began to shout at her "where's my daughter? what the bloody hell have you done with her?" They had a huge row and she had told him the truth which was the baby had been taken away for adoption and everything had been above board and it was legal there was absolutely nothing he could do about it. When Sarah had registered the baby's birth she had deliberately omitted the father's name from the child's birth certificate and so it was when she had signed the adoption papers she had once again omitted the fathers name from any of the legal documents ironically the family who had been given the baby had only lived a short distance away from where the policeman was living. Unknown to the policeman Sarah had set up the child's adoption a few weeks prior to their supposed wedding. The girls had thought their mother may have been paid, as she didn't do anything if there wasn't money involved, by the couple who had adopted the baby the couple had never been present at the flat prior to the signing of the adoption papers. The girls had only seen the woman who eventually adopted the little girl when she handed their mother a brown envelope just before the adoption papers were signed at one of the official offices in the city centre. Hence why Sarah didn't go through with the wedding because she had already completed the adoption of the policeman's baby. She had received an unknown amount of money as payment for the baby. No one would ever see the policeman again because soon after having been stood up at the registry office. He had applied to his local Police Inspector for an immediate transfer from the station he was based at and his inspector had fully understood why he had applied to leave the area and he had endorsed his request for a move. It was by now well known within the police station of what had happened to him and so he was duly transferred to a police station in the North of the city he never returned to south Liverpool. A Christian charitable organisation sometimes came to visit Sarah to drop off a bag of clothes for the children and for Chloe she would never receive anything from the bag of clothes any clothes that were left over were sold on by her mother. The money came in very handy and it went towards her drinking and her gambling habits. Chloe had never felt any love or kindness from her mother there was never any affection shown towards her but she still had an urge to please her mother and as she grew up she began to realise more and more what her mother was doing to the family and even more so how she had been treating her. It wasn't too long before Sarah once again became pregnant and nine months later a baby boy was born he was called George and when the baby was brought into the flat for the very first time Chloe was approaching thirteen and it was to be her task to make the baby's many bottles of milk and to feed him on one particular morning she hadn't had breakfast and her stomach was so sore and tender and when she was mixing the babies bottle with powdered milk she had mixed it with hot water some of the powdered milk spilled out of the container into the kitchen sink she had quickly mixed the powder in a jam jar and then added some hot water to the powder she shook it to make sure the milk powder had been thoroughly mixed in with the water. Once it had been mixed she had eagerly drunk the mixture once she had drunk it she had felt a little better as her hunger pains had subsided at least for now. The Roman Catholic church were aware of Sarah's family's situation the local priest would often visit the family and Sarah would often tell the priest to "fuck off" and to leave her alone as it wasn't a priest she had needed and certainly did not need him how to bring up her family what she needed was some money and some clothes for the children not platitudes from a priest. She had registered with a local church charity for subsistence help. Sarah was an extremely hard centred person she had shown far more love and kindness to the younger child George than she ever did to Chloe. George's father did have money but he was also a married man and at some time he had an affair with Sarah, he had his own children, his children were of the same age as Sarah's older children Chloe, Dorothy and Anne who were by now in their early teens they once went to get their hair pampered at a hairdresser it was the man's wife who owned hairdressers. At the time, she ran the hairdressers she had known Chloe and Anne, because when their half brother George was the child she would also come to see Sarah's at her flat along with her husband she had known all about her husbands "love" child to Chloe it was a very peculiar situation. He would often come to the flat and give Sarah some money for the upkeep of the boy. Sometime much later Sarah had managed to get herself a job as a live in domestic servant and a cook for a doctor in Grove Street it was a very up market part of the city and the doctor was an elderly man he lived on his own his surgery had occupied one of the much larger rooms within the House. Sarah's family had lived in rooms within the cellar area the rooms had originally been built for the domestic servants who ran the old house Anne had refused to move in with her mother and instead stayed with one of her aunts. When the children moved into the house they thought they were living in a palace and for the very first time they had real beds to sleep on and clean mattresses and clean bedding and at last there was always food on the table for the children it had seemed as though their mother was finally making a go of things and life seemed to be getting so much better. That was until Sarah began to bring men back to the rooms eventually the good doctor was informed about the strange men having been seen entering the rooms below the house. Chloe thought one of the strange men had looked a little bit like the actor "Ray Millard". Sarah had been warned previously by the Doctor regarding the rules pertaining to living in his house he had clearly laid down the rule regarding her behaviour whilst living in his home and how if she disobeyed the rules it would affect her employment with him she had been found to flouting them. She had been warned that under no uncertain terms was she was to bring any men into his house. Sarah had lied and had not taken any notice of what the doctor had said to her when she had taken up her position with the good doctor he was a no nonsense type of person and never allow anything to besmirch his reputation or his name in any way as he could not afford to be associated with anything Sarah had been up to under his roof so he had no other choice but to sack her and to evict her and of course the children from his property she only had herself to blame she had brought the whole situation she found herself in on herself. The family had to move into the home for sailors and their families based in Liverpool and as Fred had been a sailor and fisherman working in the docks and at times on the tugs and so Sarah and the children were able stay but it would mean she would have to earn her keep during the families stay at the home and once again she had found herself employed as a cook at the home. The children hated living at there but at the same time their mother had no other choice as she had to put a roof over their heads and to feed them Anne still hadn't returned to her mother for her as always it had been blinding obvious and she had realised what her mother had been up to. Eventually things got so bad at the sailor's home and so Sarah had once again upped sticks and went to live with a friend, her friend had her own family and lived on her own with her children. It was a very tight squeeze everyone was living on top of one another and eventually Sarah had found some rooms in Clive Street. It was fast approaching Christmas and living as they did the family could never afford xmas they didn't have any presents or a traditional dinner the children had realised it was the festivities because whenever they had left the flat and would see the Christmas trees and decorations in the shop windows back at the flat it had looked just like the poor living in Dickensian London would have lived. After the festive season Chloe's friends would tell her all about what Santa Claus had brought them and she would just say "yes" and would then tell them how she had received very similar presents and she would make up stories of how great her Christmas had been. She hadn't wanted to feel left out of the festivities but she was acutely aware other children could be so cruel to one another and she was frightened that they would tell everyone about her not having a traditional Christmas and would skit at her for not receiving any presents. As she was stood talking to her friends she was standing in her wellington boots and the boots had so many holes in them and some of the holes had been repaired with a puncture repair outfit with pieces of rubber having been glued over the many holes in her boots there were at least ten patches covering her boots. Once again, her mother had disappeared for night and she would reappear in the morning. The local parents had been talking about Sarah because she been seen in the local pubs and sometimes her mother's friends would talk to Chloe about her mum and of some of the places she had been seen in during the previous evening, she didn't care about what her mum was up to because she was more concerned about where her next meal would come from. Things carried on like this for many years as the children grew into adulthood the situation with their mother was becoming more obvious. As Chloe left school? she had found some work at a local bakery and whenever she collected her wages she would take them straight home to her mother and she would seize the wage packet and would hand back only a tiny amount of money to her. It was as though her mother was deliberately trying to keep Chloe down and poor that she had no real option but to rely on her. Sarah would never ever dream of taking money from her elder daughter Dorothy. It wasn't very long before young Chloe had fallen out with the manageress at the bakery and she would end up walking out of the bakery for good. The manageress knew Chloe's mum and gave her daughters severance pay that was owed, Chloe was oblivious to the severance pay and she had thought because when she had walked out of work she would not be entitled to any. It was such a cruel world in which she lived things would soon change and for the better. The day she had walked out of her job she obviously had to tell her mother of her action and her mother's response was "fuck off out of the house and don't come back until you have found yourself another job" Chloe didn't know that her mother had already known about her walking out she had only known because the manageress had handed her the severance money. Poor Chloe was still none the wiser about the money. Eventually she soon found herself a new job working at the city caterers, it was a café come cake shop. The people who worked there including the owner were aware of Chloe's upbringing only by reputation. One weekend Dorothy her elder sister had decided to ride her bicycle from Liverpool to Hull and back again and all in a weekend, she had gone to visit her Grandmother Susan who was living at Greek Street Hull. When she returned home her mother screamed at her, "where the fuck does you think you have been", Dorothy suddenly burst into tears her mother had never spoken to her like that before and yet Dorothy knew how her mother had been treating her younger sister Chloe for so many years. When she explained where she had been Sarah said, "don't you bloody go and see her ever again do you hear me?" Dorothy meekly replied, "yes mam". At the time those who knew the family had looked at Chloe and many of them had formed an opinion she was wild, feral and totally out of control and they could never understand why out of all of the children

Chloe was the only wild one but what no one knew it had been her mother Sarah who had deliberately "groomed" her to act as she did she had been living a somewhat "Cinderella" type of existence and Chloe didn't know any different all she had ever craved for was love and to feel wanted and she had tried so desperately to please her mother. What Chloe hadn't realised at the time was as she grew older her mother was becoming more and more aware her daughter would eventually meet someone and would eventually fly the nest. She was concerned her daughter would eventually come to realise there was far more to life than living in a dirty flat in abject poverty to be treated like a female version of the character "Oliver Twist". Her mother was losing what control and influence she held over her youngest daughter.

Chapter 7 – Freedom

Britain by the end of the nineteen fifties was fast approaching a new and a very dynamic decade and it would be known as the swinging sixties and Chloe was going to be part of it. Rationing had finally come to an end in 1954 and the nation was gearing up to provide goods that had been denied to the nation during the austere years of the second world war. The shops had begun to sell brightly coloured clothes and a much varied selection of fruit such as bananas they were by now arriving in the shops. Commerce was at an all time high and coffee shops were springing up in many of the larger cities and American influences were starting to flood into the country. Music and many pop groups were emerging out of the darkness. In Liverpool music was always available to the young people of the city a lot of the music within the city had emerged from the USA, Liverpool had an ear for the black music emerging from America and much of the music was purchased in America by the sailors who would then bring the music back to Liverpool on the ships that the sailors were working on they would sell the music to the various music shops in the city. One afternoon Chloe had been taking a stroll through Sefton park together with her friends she was fast approaching 19 and she was blossoming into a well balanced young woman but she hadn't lost any of her childhood cheekiness and she still possessed her sharp tongue despite everything that had happened to her as she was growing up she was still living at home with her mother and her siblings. As Chloe and her friends left the park they crossed over Aigburth Road and as they walked past a garage a couple of young men had just left the garage the two young men were apprentice motor mechanics. The girls were walking in front of them and one of the men began to whistle at the girls it was Chloe who had turned around first and she had been very cheeky towards the two men, during her young life she had grown up having been exposed to every profanity her mother could spout at her and she swore at her daily and yet Chloe had never once resorted to swearing. She may have been cheeky but she had prided herself for not swearing and taking after her mother in that respect. She had certainly made up for it with her extremely sharp wit and her sharp tongue and she certainly knew how to use it. After the whistling, the girls began to quickly walk away from the men suddenly someone grabbed hold of Chloe's arm and it had alarmed her when she looked at who had grabbed her she could see it had been the youngest of the two men. He hadn't meant any harm and as he gazed into her eyes their eyes had locked in a hypnotic stare he suddenly shouted, "this one's mine" and in that split second, they knew they had found one another. Chloe stopped struggling and stood beside him and he asked her "and what do you call yourself then lass?" "my name is Ron and not Ronald" Chloe replied "I like the name Ron my name is Chloe" just then his mate shouted "come on Ron we have to leave and we have to get a move on shift it" Ron and Chloe quickly agreed to meet up at the garage at the same time the following day, as Ron walked off, Chloe shouted "I will meet you tomorrow but it will have to be half an hour later I am at work" he shouted "ok Chloe". As Chloe walked home with her friends they giggled regarding how Chloe had been caught by young Ron, for once Chloe was seemed to be very quiet and as the two groups disappeared in to the distance Chloe turned around and waved at Ron he waved back just as he disappeared from her view. Chloe knew that she had just met someone very special. When she arrived home, her was at home she said, "Chloe its pay day tomorrow and I will need a little bit more money from you ok" Chloe looked at her mother square in the eyes and for the first time was defiant and said "no, no more mam" she had never stood up to her mother before and with that Chloe went into her bedroom. Her mother knew that Chloe had been saving some of her wages and had been placing it in a post office account her mother would have given anything to get hold of her daughter's money but Chloe had given her post office savings book to an aunt, her mother's sister, for safe keeping. Her mother was shocked at her daughter's reaction Chloe had never defied her before and had never stood up to her Chloe had wanted to buy a new dress with her next pay day to impress Ron and she certainly wasn't going to give her mother more of her hard earned cash only for her mother to waste it on the horses or her booze besides Chloe had worked extremely hard for her money and it was time that she treated herself to something nice. By refusing to give her mum more of her wages it was a warning shot to her mother Chloe had finally grown up and she felt for the first time like she was at last an adult and she had wanted the same things other young people had wanted in life. She had the same aspirations as any other young person of the day and those had included happiness and love. She had only tasted true love once before and that was when she had been evacuated during the war and had been living with Mr and Mrs Jones. Later, the same evening her mother was sat at the kitchen table she had dreaded this day it was the day when her daughter the child she had manipulated for decades would suddenly have a mind of her own. Chloe was also realising how her own mother had manipulated her as a child. The following day when Chloe was on her lunch break from work, she purchased a new dress of her choice and after work she went to meet Ron at his garage but when she arrived at the garage and went into the office the young woman who worked in the office she looked up at Chloe and said, "can I help you?" Chloe replied, "I am here to meet Ron" the woman replied, "Oh I am so sorry you have just missed him he has just left work" Chloe felt downhearted she had thought Ron may have been messing her around and besides they had only met the day before she felt so stupid to think someone would like her after just a day. She began to walk back to the dark damp flat that she had called home suddenly, she heard a voice shouting "Chloe, Chloe wait" as she looked back towards the garage she could see that it was Ron who had been shouting, he had a stupid grin on his face, Chloe thought that he looked very clean and smart in his new looking trousers, shirt and his snazzy jacket. Oh, how her heart lifted she was so happy, he gave her a kiss and they walked together towards a local café inside they chatted for hours until the early evening. Soon after their first date they would see more and more of one another, Chloe had also told him more about her upbringing Ron also told her all about his own family. Chloe soon realised just how different their lives really were. Chloe was beginning to think her upbringing hadn't been so normal it had soon dawned upon her why her mother had controlled her knowledge is all powerful. It wasn't long before Sarah had got to hear about her daughter walking out with a posh lad from Fernhill Street Toxteth. One afternoon Chloe had arrived home and a bald man was just leaving the flat and he had roughly pushed past Chloe he seemed to be in such a hurry Chloe had never seen the strange man before and when she walked into the flat she asked her mother "what was that man doing here" her mother replied, "oh I don't know he said he was lost and wanted to know the directions to a pub" Chloe thought "a very likely story". The next day when she met Ron he seemed to be very angry she could tell straight away that he wasn't happy at all. He went on to explain about a bald headed man who had approached him outside the garage the man had tried to warn him off from seeing her again but he had grabbed the man and had told him to fuck off as he was going to marry Chloe and if the man knew what was good for him he would stay away from the pair of them. Other people in the garage had heard the commotion outside and a couple of the mechanics came out onto the main road with large spanners the man was last seen running down the road with his tail between his legs. Ron said to Chloe that he thought her mother may have had something to do with the attack, because the man knew too much about the pair of them she said to Ron "did you say he had a bald head", Ron replied "yes he did have a bald patch why do you know him?", she said "no, but I know my mother does". They took a walk into Sefton park and it was such a lovely day she thought that it was high time she told Ron more details regarding her upbringing and of course her past and when she had finished pouring her heart out he said, "look Chloe that was all in the past we could have a great future together" she then told him about seeing a bald man leaving her mother's flat the previous day, possibly the same man who had tried to warn him off from seeing her. Ron had pointed out to her he had suspected her mother was trying to interfere in her life and it had to stop and her future could be with him. Ron vowed never to meet her mother as he might not be responsible for his actions. She looked Ron in the eyes and said, "you know when you told me you told that horrible man you were going to marry me, did you mean what you had said?" Ron replied yes I did sweetheart and I meant every word I said" they sat down on a bench and had a cuddle and kissed. Ron invited her to his parents' house for a Sunday lunch, Chloe said "I have never had a proper Sunday lunch Ron" Ron laughed and he replied "oh Chloe you have so much to learn" and as soon as she arrived home she spoke to her mother about the horrible bald man and she went on to tell her that he had tried to scare her boyfriend off from seeing her again and her mother had tried to deny any knowledge of any bald man she said she didn't know what she was talking about and her mother then tried to muddy the waters by pointing out to her there were thousands of bald headed men in Liverpool. Chloe said to her "well mam it didn't work and whatever it is you are trying to do, if anything it has only made me and Ron even stronger we have strong feelings for one another". That evening her mother lay in bed thinking that her worst fears were about to come true. The following morning was a Saturday and Chloe had gone off to work as usual and that lunchtime after work she went shopping and had brought some new clothes to wear for when she visited Ron's parents. That Saturday afternoon she met up with Ron in town and she was carrying a shopping bag it contained her new clothes Ron said "oh yes and who are you getting all dressed up for then"? they laughed and kissed she said "you know why cheeky" and they went to get a bite to eat and once they had eaten they caught a bus and got off at Park Road and then walked up to North Hill Street and then into Fernhill Street they soon arrived at his parent's house they entered a small enclosed court yard through a set of double wooden doors. They then entered a large house and went into the kitchen where Ron had made a nice pot of tea Chloe was sat at the kitchen table and thought to herself "wow this is such a world away from where I live it's a paradise and it feels so warmly and loving", Chloe became a little over excited and became a slightly louder and said "Ron this is so lovely thank you so much" he replied "Chloe just be a little quite our dad is upstairs asleep" she said "oh ok Ron anyway why is your dad asleep at this time of day"? Ron explained his dad worked nights as he worked as a cleaner at the local bus depot" Just then Ron's dad Cyril walked into the kitchen, he sat down at the kitchen table and said "ah Ron you have company, hello young lady I'm Ron's dad Cyril" Chloe replied "hello I hope you don't mind me being in your house" he replied "no not at all it is nice to see our Ron with some company" Ron said "dad this is Chloe" Ron poured a cup of tea for his dad. Sunday had soon come around and Chloeret was dressed in her new clothes and her mother had immediately noticed she was dressed up and she said to her, "where the fuck do you bloody think you are going to dressed up like that all hoity totty" Chloe curtly replied "out". With that she walked out of the flat and as she walked down the road a few of her friends had seen her all dressed up and her friends were off to a local pub with their boyfriends one of her friends shouted over to her "where are you off to Chloe you look fantastic" she replied, "I'm off to my Ron's house" her friend replied, "good on you enjoy". She eventually arrived at Ron's house and knocked on the front door eventually a very tall lady answered the door Chloe gulped as she had recognised the lady standing before her it had been when she was a child she had been in the area very close by to Ron's house and that's where she had recognised the lady stood in the doorway it had been from all those years ago, "the woman said you must be our Ron's new girlfriend?" and she replied, "yes I suppose I must be" she hadn't been too sure how much Ron had told his mum regarding the relationship as they walked into the kitchen Chloe sat down at the kitchen table. Ron said, "mam this is my latest girlfriend Chloe" he turned to her and said, "Chloe this is our mam Dorothy or should I say Dolly" his mum scowled at him and laughed loudly Dolly said, "Chloe you can call me Dolly" Cyril said, "she must like you as she has never asked anyone outside of the family to call her Dolly before" they all laughed and Chloe soon felt so much at ease but she could tell that Dolly ruled the roost. As Dolly began to speak she looked very serious and she addressed Chloe directly "I hope young lady that you are not going to mess our Ron around regarding the pair of you getting engaged and married" Chloe looked horrified she hadn't realised that Ron had gone and told his parents so much Chloe she was about to say something when Ron piped up and said "oh yes Chloee will you marry me" She was a little shocked at first and said "yes Ron of course I will" Ron's dad, Cyril, very rarely said anything, he was a man of very few words, but on this occasion he was over the moon and he quickly popped out to an off licence and when he returned he had brought back some drinks. Chloe said that she didn't drink but she would love a glass of ice cold lemonade. They all sat down and ate their Sunday lunch and it had soon turned into an engagement party. When Ron had walked Chloe back to her mother's flat she said, "Ron would you like to meet my mum now?" Ron refused the offer as he could not meet a person who had been treating her the way her mother had he just couldn't justify being nice towards her mother. She gave him a kiss and climbed the stairs to the flat Ron began his walk home and as she had entered the flat her mother was stood in the kitchen she was dressed in her smart clothes she was obviously about to go out for the evening, she said to Chloe "you are going to have to look after George tonight" Chloe calmly replied "ok but let me tell you this much from now on you will have to find yourself another babysitter and soon" her mother snapped "why" it was at this point Chloe could not contain herself she went on to explain to her mother that she was engaged to be married her mother went ballistic "for fuck sake I haven't got time to argue with you right now" and so off she went and out for the night. She had felt so good and so liberated for once in her life she had met someone who had cared about her and had loved her for who she was and right from the start she had been open and honest with Ron regarding her past life and he had accepted her for who she was and he had always said it was the future that mattered and everyone had a past. The following morning over breakfast her mother had returned from another one of her nights out most of the family were having breakfast and all of a sudden their mother began to scream at all of them "your fucking sister is leaving us and she is going to get married to a toffy nosed git and when she fuck's off you can blame her and not me when I can't afford to buy food or pay the rent" Anne spoke up and said "mam leave her alone I shall be leaving soon and it will be very soon as I am getting married to my "Bob"". Soon after Chloe had told her mother she was getting married she had decided to leave the family home and had moved in to Ron's parent's home she would never go back to her mother's house only with her children and only for the odd visit.

Chapter 8 - Family

Living at Ron's parent's house wasn't an easy thing for Chloe to have undertaken, Dolly had started to interfere more and more in the young couple's lives, Chloe had a lifetime of interference from her own mother, admittedly it was much worse than Dolly, but it was still the feeling of someone trying to control her everyday life. At the time, Chloe had been thinking to herself she had seen Dolly somewhere else and one day the penny suddenly dropped. She soon realised it was on a summers day when she was about fourteen she had come up to the Toxteth region to "go shopping", as a child Chloe had looked upon the area where Ron's family was living as a much posher area of Liverpool than where she lived, in her head she was living in the lowest of the low areas of Liverpool, in her mind upper Toxteth was full of rich families and one summers afternoon she was in the area. On that day, it was extremely hot some households had left the front doors open to allow cooler and fresh air to permeate the house. Chloe's beady eyes had immediately spotted a house with the front door it was left wide open, she stood on the pavement in front of the house, she could just make out some children's shoes in the hallway. She had looked around to make sure no one was looking, she had waited for a few minutes to ensure there wasn't any movement within the hallway of the house, when she had been satisfied no one was around and the coast was definitely clear, she was taking such a risk if she was caught, but utter desperation makes people do some very desperate things, Chloe suddenly shot up the steps into the house, her heart was pounding, she grabbed a pair of children's shoes and ran back down the steps and ran as hard as she could into another street, it was the same street where Ron lived in, and who was stood on the corner of the street was Dolly,

Ron's mother, she was chatting to another woman, Dolly stood with her arms folded across her chest. Chloe had calmly and had nonchalantly walked passed the pair of them and carried on walking down the street, once she had reached the end of the street she ran home as fast as her legs could take her, at the same time hugging the shoes close to her chest, her heart had felt as though it would suddenly burst through her tiny chest. When she arrived home her mother had taken the shoes from her and had sold them to the local pawn shop, the shoes were far too good for Chloe to wear. When Chloe had told Ron about this, and that she had seen his mother as a child and on the day, she had "borrowed" the shoes. Dolly was very good to Chloe when she stayed at her house, but Dolly became far too interfering for Chloe's liking. Chloe had craved her own life with Ron and a family of her own. Chloe and Ron had eventually decided to move out of his parent's house and to find themselves a place of their own, Ron had fully understood why Chloe had wanted to move from his parent's house and had agreed with Chloe to leave, he was fully supportive of her. Cyril worked night shifts and if he wasn't working on a night shift he would be getting up for work, to work on a spilt shift at the local bus depot, he would leave for work at all god forsaken hours of the day. The reason Cyril worked and had preferred the night shifts it was because he was in constant pain in his left shoulder and arm. During world war two, he had been attacked while he was on guard duty in Palestine and one evening he was patrolling a large military vehicle park. On this particular guard duty it started off just like any other mundane duty, there was nothing special about carrying out this particular guard duty, but during his stint on duty, he had been attacked, during the attack he had managed to unslung his rifle from his shoulder just as one of the attackers had pulled a knife and attacked Cyril, he had managed to turn his body slightly during the struggle and during the struggle the assailants knife sliced through his heavy trench coat and had sliced through the coat and the knife had plunged deeply into his left shoulder the blade of the knife was razor sharp and had sliced down the flesh and muscle of his left arm and at the same time he had managed to raise the general alarm, the assailants immediately fled and had managed to blend into the night and melt into the tiny streets surrounding the camp, the authorities had believed the group who had attacked Cyril was a well-known Jewish terrorist organisation. The group had been after the many military vehicles to use in their campaign against the British Army in Palestine, at the time the group were forever stealing British Military Vehicles, rifles munitions and equipment. Cyril had spent many weeks in hospital recovering from his serious injuries and there had been severe damage to the nerves in his shoulder and his arm, hence the job with the bus depot. Cyril was saddened by the news of Ron and Chloe moving out of his house, but once again he fully understood the reasons why, it was him that had to live with Dolly. He had enjoyed the company of Chloe in the house and the chats together. Ron had managed to find a flat and the rent had been within the couple's small budget. Ron was unaware of Chloe's savings, Chloe hadn't wanted to go through the feelings of being poor ever again, hence squirrelling away every spare penny that she earnt. At the same time, Chloe, didn't have too much to do with her mother, the more she was away from her mother the more she learnt so much more about the world around her and it helped so much she was living with a man who cared for her and was showing her there was a different life away from her mother, she would meet up frequently with her sisters Anne and Dorothy. It was during a meeting with the pair of them when Anne had broken the news regarding one of their half-brothers Mark he had recently passed away in a local work house. Mark was known in the family for his very heavy drinking, he would also walk the streets of Liverpool and he was a well known tramp. Anne went on to tell Chloe he had recently been buried in a pauper grave, Chloe never looked on Mark, Mildred or George as part of the "family" to her they were "Love children" and weren't related to her, a lot of her feelings were formed during her early life and having been treated like dirt by her own mother and yet the "Love children" were very well cared for. The girl Mildred, the policeman's daughter, who had been adopted. Anne had told Chloe that Mildred had recently been in contact with her, Chloe wasn't at all interested. George had become a successful lawyer within the city, and once again Chloe wasn't interested in anything Anne had to say about her half brothers and sister, Chloe had blocked out any thoughts or feelings towards the "Love children" it was now her turn to live life and enjoy life with her beloved Ron and finally look forward to her future with the man she loved, it was the only way she could live and move on from her awful past. Chloe and Ron eventually married at the local registry office, Ron's parents and family were in attendance, Chloe had also invited her sisters to the ceremony, but not her mother. It was a year later when Chloe had fallen pregnant with their son Gordon, Ron and Chloe were over the moon their baby boy was born healthy. Ron and Chloe soon realised immediately after the birth of their son, they would have to find some better accommodation and a well-paid job, things were about to turn for the better for the young family it was Nineteen fifty nine and Ron had been called up to the Armed Forces, in the Army, the country still had National Service all males had to carry out a period of National Service in any one of the Armed Forces, it meant once again yet more upheaval for the young family, Chloe was fine as soon as Ron had explained the situation to her. At the time, there were lots of people and friends of Chloe's whose boyfriends and their husbands had been called up to carry out their period of National Service, National Service was for a period of eighteen months. Ron was also required to carry out his basic training at the Royal Army Ordnance Corps Depot, RAOC, at the time the Depot was based in Portsmouth Hampshire. The RAOC was the Army's Ordnance department providing such stores as staples, nuts, bolts to ammunition and so much more, you name it they would provide it. There was a second "arm" of the corps which trained staff clerks and help to provide the administrative support to the Army's staff Officers at each Army Headquarters. Ron had trained in the stores section of the Corps. To Chloe Ron was her rock, her education he helped to educate her on most daily aspects of her life, she was clueless, she became a little lost with Ron being away, but she was tenacious character and just got on with her life. During Ron's absence, she had decided to take Gordon and two of her friends to visit Mrs Jones in Weaverham Chloe hadn't seen "Ma Jones" since 1945 it had been some eleven years since leaving Ma Jones's loving home, to Chloe it had seemed a lifetime ago. When she arrived at Mr Jones's house she was about to open the gate that lead to the house when Ma Jones opened the door and met Chloe on the garden path, after such a long gap, she had immediately recognised Chloe and she hugged Chloe on the foot path, she had always showered Chloe with love and affection, something Chloe's own mother had never once showed her, they all stepped inside and into the parlour they had tea and some of Ma Jones's freshly baked cakes. Chloe handed baby Gordon over to Ma Jones, Gordon with his long curly blonde hair, Chloe went on to explain about how she and Ron had met and got married and his National Service commitments. This was the last time Chloe ever saw Ma Jones, she informed Chloe that Mr Jones had died not too long after she had returned to

The Journey

Liverpool. Chloe travelled back to Liverpool by train, the return journey had brought back so many memories, they arrived back to the smog filled city. Meanwhile as Ron was undertaking his basic training he was missing Chloe and had been wishing his days away, the soldiers had various briefings about the conflicts the National Service recruits might have to serve in and it covered many parts of the world and in many parts of the then British Empire some of the soldiers who had been briefing the conscripts had combat experience in the Korean war. Much of the trainings consisted of square bashing and the bulling of boots and making the brass on their uniforms shiny. The instructors were Regular full time soldiers, they knew most of the National Service men would leave as soon as their eighteen months' service was up. Ron could see there could be a future career in the Army for him. At the time, there were many rumours about National Service possibly being phased out within the next year. Ron was called to see his Company Commander a Major Brown. Major Brown informed Ron that he was very impressed by Ron's conduct during his basic training he thought Ron was doing extremely well during training. He asked Ron if he had ever thought about enlisting into the regular Army, at this stage it was more of a gentle enquiry by the Company Commander, the Army knew without the National Servicemen the Army would considerably shrink from its current size and would need to persuade some of the conscripted recruits into the Regular Army, they had to recruit them prior to them having completed their eighteen months of conscription. Ron asked the Major, "If I do agree to enrolling into the Regular Army would my family be able to move with me, and would I be entitled to a married quarter?" the Major had obviously been handed a briefing pack with such questions and the answers when attempting to enroll conscripts into the regular Army, he replied "yes of course". Ron told the

Family

Major that he would have answer for him in a day or two, he knew he had to speak to Chloe on the phone to get her views, during his basic training he wasn't yet entitled to any leave, apart from compassionate leave. So, over the next two days he spoke to Chloe on the communal telephone, In the accommodation block, the recruits had access to a communal phone Ron had written the number down prior to his bout of military training. Chloe had agreed to the idea of him serving in the regular Army, she knew the family must improve their lot and Ron's opportunity wasn't just a job it was a career move with huge promotion prospects. After Chloe's agreement Ron applied for a Commanding Officers interview and informed the Major of his decision, and immediately after the interview Ron was moved out of his current accommodation block and moved into another block, where there were about fifty other recruits it transpired that they had agreed to serve in the Regular full time Army, over the next few days they had to fill in and sign new contracts agreeing to serve in the Regular Army, their training had also changed there wasn't so much drill on the parade square, the training consisted of far more Range work and the recruits were drilled in the different armaments the British Army operated and they had far more technical training, after a month or two Ron was to attend a technical stores course at Bicester the biggest surprise for him was being handed a two week leave pass prior to attending his course and of course his wages were going to be so much better. On his leave Ron had left Bicester and got a train to Liverpool and arrived just as Liverpool was waking up to a bright sunny morning, Ron walked to their flat on the way he purchased a newspaper from a street vendor, life felt very good for Ron in his mind he knew all of them were on a path to a much better life, he had let himself into the flat Chloe was already up and feeding Gordon, she hadn't realised Ron had been given any leave, she was shocked when Ron had suddenly walked into the flat, she initially thought he had left the Army and gone Absent Without Leave, AWOL, she was more concerned he would be arrested for being Absent without leave, Ron had to calm her down and he went on to explain why he was back home, he also had some extra money on him, Ron would have a flutter on the horses or play the odd game of cards for money. He sat Chloe down at the kitchen table and began to explain in so much more detail about both of their decision for Ron to sign on with the Regular Army, and about the possibility of serving overseas and more than likely he would be working in post war West Germany, in 1955 West Germany had joined The North Atlantic Treaty Organisation, NATO, it was only ten years after the ending of the second world war. Britain was also a member of NATO, there was a requirement to station British forces in West Germany to protect West Germany from a Russian invasion. Chloe understood everything Ron had told her, the only question she had was, would she and baby Gordon be joining him in Germany Ron confirmed to her that all three of them would be together, The Army would be providing housing called Married quarters. It was all Chloe needed to hear, she was very happy she knew her life was already changing and for the better with Ron. She knew her life would change forever and she was so happy. Ron said to Chloe they would need to go around to his parent's house first in the morning to let them know he was back in the city and to prepare them for the news that he may have to move to West Germany. Chloe told Ron he was more than welcome to come with her to her mother's flat to tell her of the news, Ron declined the offer, he had already told Chloe many years ago, he wouldn't go near her mother it was all due to the way she had treated Chloe as a child. Chloe arrived at her mother's flat and as soon as she walked through the door she knew it had been a big mistake to visit her mum, she wanted so much to introduce her mother to her very first grandchild and to tell her that she would be living overseas in West Germany. Chloe chose a Saturday to go and visit her mother, the weather was nice and sunny it was late summer, as soon as she walked into her mother's flat she immediately knew nothing had changed much since leaving her mother. The black and white Television was switched on and blaring away and the living room was thick with cigarette smoke the sound of a horse racing commentary was blaring from the television also sat in one of the grubby chairs in the living room was a priest he was also smoking a cigarette and was drinking a glass of stout. Her mother said "Chloe you know father O'Malley do you remember him when you were a little one", this wasn't what Chloe wanted to see, her head was spinning, it only went to confirm she was so lucky to be with Ron and she just wanted to protect Gordon from her past, her mother may have been living in a new flat, but the atmosphere was the same, as she had remembered it as a child, she just wanted to bolt out of the flat it was just too much for her to handle. Chloe politely said hello to the priest, her mother held Gordon but she immediately gave him back to Chloe, her mother was sat on a grotty looking couch with a cigarette hanging from her lips, supping on a glass of stout, the priest was glued to the TV and for that matter Sarah her mother was as well, she was swearing like a trooper at the race coverage on the TV. Her horse had lost the race, but to Chloe it was like living back at home as a child again, when she was a child they didn't own a TV but it didn't stop her mother and her horse racing she would listen to the horse racing on a wireless. Chloe told her mother that she and Ron would be living in West Germany for a while, her mother hissed "what the fuck do want to be doing that for, it is full of foreigners?" Chloe said her goodbyes and soon left the flat, her mother didn't bother to see her to the door, as Chloe pushed Gordon home in his pram Chloe thought to herself "I am so lucky to have Ron and Gordon in my life". She immediately knew that she had made the right decision together with Ron, her life wasn't going to be in Liverpool it was going to be with Ron and wherever he served in the world. As far as Chloe and Ron were concerned they had made a new life together, they were leaving Liverpool behind to begin a totally different life, for Chloe it was now her time to enjoy what the world had to offer, to leave the dirt-poor world she lived in before getting married to Ron. They were very happy with their lot. It was time for the pair of them to accomplish something of their lives and to live and breathe with one another are a loving couple, the marriage was a partnership of total commitment to one another. It was time to make something of their lives and for their young family. For Chloe, this was the most important thing she had ever done in her life and she wasn't scared to face the world head on, she was a woman of very strong character, it was soon time for the world to be introduced to Chloe.

Chapter 9 – A Brighter Future

Soon after Gordon was born Ron had been informed about where he was going to be serving. Even though Chloe had informed her mother about him and that he was to be stationed in West Germany she hadn't a clue where West Germany was. He was to be "posted" to West Germany and he was going to be based in the city of Dortmund. When Ron had tried his very best to explain to Chloe where Dortmund was she had responded by saying "yes lovely Ron it sounds really nice" Ron knew Chloe didn't have a clue about what he had told her she had only been to Weaverham in Cheshire and to New Brighton on the Wirral peninsular. Whenever she had to travel to New Brighton from Liverpool she and her friends would travel across the River Mersey on the Liverpool ferry it was the limit to her travels. Ron went on to explain that he would have to travel to Dortmund on his own and would send for her as soon as he had been allocated a military house. She had understood he had to travel ahead and she couldn't wait to join him in West Germany with their son soon after Ron's news she had sat in the flat pondering exactly where Dortmund was in the world. Her geography wasn't the best she had resorted to asking a few of her friends where West Germany was one had told her it was in France and another had said it was somewhere in the South of England. Chloe went to visit Ron's parents she had told them of the news about Ron and Dolly said, "ah Chloe we already know Chloe, Ron has already spoken to me and Cyril it was soon after he had phoned you and he had said that you might come and visit" Chloe had pushed the pushchair into the hallway Gordon was fast asleep it was very awkward to wheel the pram into the kitchen. Cyril was already sat in the kitchen having a mug of tea he looked up at Chloe and began to speak and it was very rare for him to speak "how are you sweetheart?" She said her normal hello's she looked down at Cyril and asked him "where is Dortmund" he explained it was an industrial city in the heart of West Germany he also explained where West Germany was in Europe and it was next door to France. Chloe enquired would she have to get a train to travel there Cyril informed her that Ron would sort out the travel arrangements and he said she may have to travel by ferry of even fly to get there. She thought about what Cyril had said and she replied, "I have travelled by train it was when I was evacuated during the war" Cyril laughed and Dolly said, "you will be ok Chloe Ron will most probably be able to take some leave and bring you and Gordon back to Germany with him". She replied, "oh yes that will be much better I shall mention it to Ron when he next contacts me". It wasn't too long after Ron had arrived in West Germany and he had been allocated a nice Army house it was a 2 bed roomed house with a garden. He had travelled to Liverpool to help move Chloe and the baby back with him to Dortmund and it was to be the start of Chloe's various travels across the world. When Chloe first saw the house in West Germany she was totally awe struck as she had never lived in a house before and not only that it had a garden it was at this point she knew life would start to be kinder towards her as she had deserved some happiness in her life after a life of poverty. It wasn't too long before she had fallen pregnant again and had another son Phillip and then 18 months later Ron and Chloe had another son Stuart. For the pair life was so good and Ron was receiving a regular wage packet and the family was housed all care of his employers. Chloe would often look at her 3 boys and think how lucky she was and her sons were safe and had a roof over their heads she was extremely grateful. The couple were based at many locations within West Germany the family had enjoyed their time in West Germany and on some occasions when Ron had to move from one Military base to another on his own waiting for a Military house to be made available. Chloe and the family would have to travel back to Liverpool she and the children would stay with her in laws the boys would attend St Silas's school in Toxteth, for the boys it was just another adventure. Their play area after school and at the weekends were the various parks scattered around the Toxteth area the parks were Princess park and Sefton Park sometimes if it was a weekend or a school holiday the boys and their friends would travel as far afield as Otterspool Park. Chloe had become so used to living in a house with a garden and she was soon feeling extremely cooped up living at Ron's parent's house. On some occasions, the boy's cousins and their parents lived in and around their grandparents' house. They were always in and out of one another's houses, except our gran's house as they knew full well not to mess around in her house. When Ron's boys stayed at his parents place they would sleep in the attic and it was extremely cramped. Sometimes they would have to sleep in the same bed with some of their cousins. Cyril had his workshop in another part of the attic. He wouldn't let the brothers Phillip and Stuart into his workshop since Stuart was far too young and Phillip was always touching things and breaking them. Gordon was allegedly the most sensible one out the 3! he was very interested in what his grandad would make he would normally make working models of boats and aircraft he enjoyed listening to his grandad's stories of how he made the models. He made warships and aeroplanes from scratch and he would put engines into the models and they were all in working order. Whenever Chloe moved to Liverpool she would sometimes visit her mother and at the time Sarah was living in a block of flats close to the Dingle area and the flat was very clean looking and it had a bathroom and a working toilet and other modern facilities. On one occasion when she was visiting her mother she had taken the 3 boys with her and her brother Peter was visiting he was a bit of a loose cannon. While he was playing with the boys he had grabbed Phillip and tied him to a chair to shut him up Gordon and Stuart were laughing at Phillip all tied up. Chloe didn't often take the boys to visit their gran and as the boys grew up they knew there was something seriously wrong between their mother and their gran over the years small snippets of information would slip into a conversation it had only made the boys more inquisitive about her childhood and sometimes she would let slip something but she would never expand on what she had let slip as would like to keep some things to herself and over time if she had let her story slip out she would suddenly clam up. There were some things she wouldn't even tell her beloved Ron as she had felt so ashamed of some of the physical abuse metered out to her by her mother and she knew that he would become very angry about it all. The children knew their mother had a very hard time growing up and because she wouldn't tell them until they themselves were adults. As small children, they were read stories and nursery rhymes by their mother to other families reading stories and nursery rhymes was a normal everyday part of growing up but for the boy's mother it was such a massive issue as she still couldn't read or write very well and so whenever she didn't know a word she would replace the word or a sentence with "trala la" As the children attended school it was glaring obvious to the teachers the boys didn't know that many children's stories or nursery rhymes. It is well known in the family how the boys still struggle a little with some nursery rhymes certainly without having to read the rhyme from a book. Life became even better for the family and Chloe and Ron had completed what they had set out to do to give their family a chance in life for both it had meant leaving their families behind in Liverpool, for Chloe it hadn't been an issue or a wrench as it enabled the boys to have the best start in life. It was a far better future for them than their mother had endured and she didn't want her boys to end up the way she had. She was very determined her young family would never have to experience the life she had experienced. The boys had realised at a very early age their mother was slightly different to other mums and it wasn't in a bad way; she had some very peculiar habits and ideas which have rubbed off onto all three of the boys. For instance, in Dortmund things had started off as an ordinary day. The family were visiting a large park at the zoo in Dortmund, West Germany. Gordon was on a scooter, Phillip could walk but he had been well and truly strapped into asset of reigns he was after all the mischievous one out of all 3 of them. Stuart was in his pram. Gordon was merrily riding around on his scooter weaving in and out of the flower beds. As he rode back to where he had last seen his mother, she had vanished. But he hadn't been too surprised as his mother would often meander off in her own world and she still does. He rode around the park for what seemed like ages and it was at this point he began to panic. He had decided to track back towards the zoo entrance, thinking she may have realised she was one son short. It was the most logical spot to look for her but she was not there. Even at the age of five he found he was trying to be analytical. He was eventually stopped by a park warden who took him into an office; the warden spoke to Gordon in German. He had immediately realised that he was English and had called the Police. At some point, someone who could speak English announced over the public-address system in English and in German announcing there was a lost little boy and he was safe at the warden's office. Gordon was asked what his mother's name was, and he said, 'mummy and Phillip and Stuart'.

I think he might have confused the police they might have thought that one of his brothers was in fact his dad. His mother eventually responded and came to collect him. The boys had never felt hampered or embarrassed by their mother's lack of education, far from it, she was their mother and she thought the world of her "three boys". All 3 boys eventually went on to do amazing things with their lives far beyond Chloe and Ron's wildest dreams. Their eldest son Gordon struggled at school as he was never going to be an academic it wasn't too long before Phillip had joined Gordon at school and he did very well at school Stuart soon followed his elder brothers and he excelled at school so much so that he passed his eleven plus with such ease. After school, all three brothers had joined the Army and it hadn't been an urge or a dream of any of them to follow in their father's footsteps in fact far from it. Phillip had joined the Royal Signals Apprentice college in Harrogate as a junior leader. At the age of 16 Gordon was learning to be a bricklayer but because of his father Ron having to move around with the Military Gordon's foray into the building trade had soon ended abruptly. It was 1976 and the Labour government of Harold Wilson and Jim Callaghan had virtually brought the country to its knees there was very little work and by now Gordon was fast approaching 19 and he had recently met a nice young lady with whom he would later marry but at the time he needed a stable career and so reluctantly he had decided to join the Army and he too enlisted into the Royal Signals. A few years later Stuart had also enlisted into the Army and yes you have guessed it into the Royal Signals. When they enlisted all 3 of the brothers had travelled the world and had seen action in many conflicts and wars over the last forty years. Stuart went on to become a senior officer in the Royal Signals and went on to do very well for himself and during his service in the Army he was honoured by the Queen with an OBE,

Order of the British Empire. Phillip went on to become an exceedingly successful business man. He had worked very hard to get where he was. Gordon eventually left the Army and not before he had been awarded an MBE, member of the British Empire. He went on to become a skilled IT operative, Information Technology. After leaving the IT industry he became a writer. It is ironic that all 3 sons became very successful. Chloe and Ron were very proud of what their children had achieved in life. She didn't really understand just how successful her sons had become but she was so proud of all 3 of them. There is a touch of sadness in that Chloe's beloved Ron had suddenly passed away at a very young age of 68 which is no age at all. Initially she didn't think she could survive without him as he would do everything for her. Her life had seemed bereft without him but there was one thing in her life keeping her going and it was her sons she had their love and the love of her lovely extended family. Chloe's traits are well known within the family even down to her great grandchildren. Without her grit and steely determination, she would never have had survived her childhood. Her journey is very much ongoing and the family journey had started with a young man who had started out on his epic journey on a cold morning departing from a remote group of Islands, The Faroe Islands. Peter would have been so proud to know how his journey and his hard work would eventually lead to his great grandchildren having fulfilled lives. Peter could not have foreseen what his decision to leave the Faroe Islands would have on his future generations. His legacy still lives on through the generations who have followed him. He could never have envisaged members of his family would eventually become part of British society and members of his family would also be honoured by the Head of the British Monarchy that is where there is some irony as they are of German heritage. For a man to be killed because of his accent and his place of birth all because of some very ignorant people over a hundred years ago. Peter would have been even more proud of his granddaughter Chloe having left a life of poverty behind her and having given birth to 3 sons and to then successfully raising 3 well balanced sons'. There is a sense of irony in Peter's story because on the 16th March 1917 he was found floating in one of the many docks in Liverpool. His death had been very suspicious to say the least and the authorities of the day had enough evidence to prove he had been murdered but there hadn't been enough evidence to identify the perpetrators and to have convicted them of this most heinous of crimes. It had always been suspected he had been murdered because he was a foreigner a German. Britain and Germany at the time were at war and it was very highly likely someone had taken revenge on Peter possibly because a relative had been killed on the western front in France, we shall never know. On the 4th June 1917, the same year as Peter was murdered King George V instituted the honours system in Great Britain and three generations later two members of his own family were honoured by the Monarch Her Majesty Queen Elizabeth II. The same year Peter had been found dead the then King George V had decided to change the Royal Families surname due to anti German feeling in 1917. The King had made momentous decision to change the Royal Families name from the German surname of Saxe-Coburg-Gotha to Windsor. 1917 has many connections with Peter and the sad thing is he had lost his life. The then Royal family only had to change their surname. It was a year in which had changed Fred's destiny and ultimately his own daughter Chloe's destiny. To this very day she is prone to be woken out of a deep sleep by her reoccurring nightmares of her childhood. The memories have never faded with age or have left her memories have impacted on the way she now looks on life. In the 21st century

171

one cannot imagine a childhood growing up in such extreme poverty and the deprivation it is totally alien to today's society. It can only be a good thing that within one generation Chloe has managed to escape and build herself a new life and for generations to come. After such an awful upbringing Chloe was determined her own family would never have to suffer the way she did. There is one last thing that happened to Chloe and it was when her mother had passed away on hearing the news of her mother's death she had cried and had shed many tears for her mother or was it because the one last vesture of her past life had passed on by. As the saying goes blood is thicker than water.

Made in the USA
Columbia, SC
22 June 2018